850

Contents

Maps

TASK
FORCE
57

THE BRITISH PACIFIC FLEET
1944-1945

———o———

Peter C. Smith

WILLIAM KIMBER

First published by
WILLIAM KIMBER & CO. LIMITED
6 Queen Anne's Gate, London S.W.1

© 1969 William Kimber & Co. Limited

SBN 7183 0251 6

MADE AND PRINTED IN GREAT BRITAIN BY PURNELL & SONS, LTD.
PAULTON (SOMERSET) AND LONDON

List of Illustrations

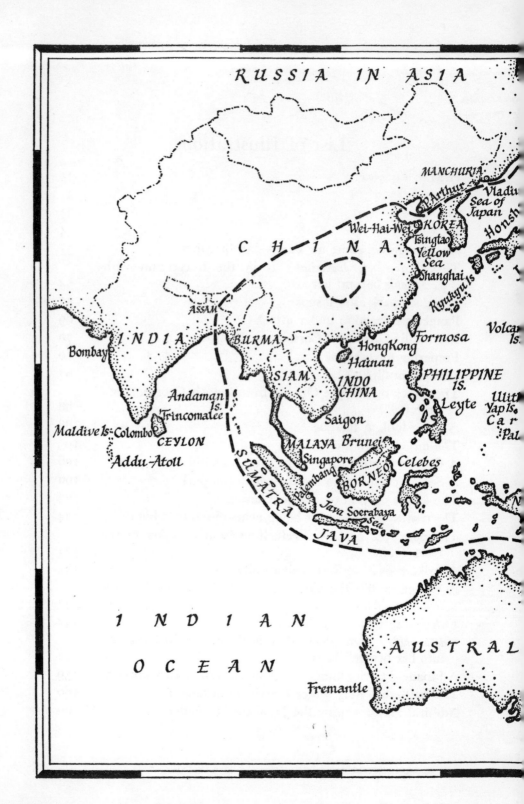

Sakhalin

Attu · Kiska
Aleutian Islands

P A C I F I C

Bonin Is.

oJima   Marcus I
                          Midway Is

O C E A N · : Hawaiin Is

Marianas Is.   Wake Is.

oGuam   Marshall
ne Islands   Islands

Truk Is.

Gilbert Is.

Rabaul
A
Port   Solomon Is.
Moresby   Guadalcanal

Tokelau

N.Samoa

The
ASIAN and
PACIFIC
BATTLEGROUND

Approximate
Japanese gains

Sydney

NEW
ZEALAND

Em

Nothing in the world, nothing that you may think or dream of, or anyone may tell you; no arguments however specious, no appeals however seductive must lead you to abandon that naval supremacy on which the life of our country depends.

WINSTON SPENCER CHURCHILL

FOR MY PARENTS

Foreword

by

Admiral of the Fleet Lord Fraser of North Cape, G.C.B., K.B.E.

This book describes ably and very well the successes and difficulties of the British Pacific Fleet. When I arrived as C.-in-C. in December 1944 it seemed a formidable task. I was responsible to the British Admiralty, 12,000 miles away, for the Fleet and its supplies; to the Australian and New Zealand Governments for our considerable local interests; and I was to come under the operational command of that great American Admiral, Admiral Nimitz, at Honolulu. But the co-operation of all concerned made it seem simple.

The Australian Government placed their efficient dockyard at our disposal, added to which there was the extreme kindliness and hospitality of the Australian people to which the British sailor when not fighting was not lacking in response! The New Zealanders provided the valuable contribution of their Fleet Air Arm pilots.

At sea I had two distinguished and experienced Admirals, Rawlings and Vian, and on shore looking after our supplies Admiral Daniel in Melbourne and Admiral Fisher at Manus responsible for the Fleet Train, the only means of keeping our Fleet supplied at sea.

The latter was perhaps our greatest headache. With the shortage of shipping it comprised an odd assortment of modern and elderly ships involving many nationalities but all doing their best.

And then Admiral Nimitz turning his blind eye to Washington would always help us out in emergencies.

It is only by dedication to the task (at which the sailor is good), co-operation and leadership that success can be achieved. I wish we had the same to-day.

East Molesey,
June, 1969

Fraser of North Cape

Introduction

by

Admiral Sir Michael Denny, G.C.B., C.B.E., D.S.O.

This account of Task Force 57, although in detail it only covers a period of about a year, is really the whole story of the Royal Navy's operations as a major carrier force. It was the first time that carriers had dominated the conduct of a campaign and even the most modern battleships, such as *King George V*, appeared in a secondary role. The battles in the Pacific were fought at ranges of 200 miles or more and opposing ships seldom closed to gun ranges.

I was fortunate in that, between the wars, I had served with the Home and Mediterranean fleets where the carrier squadrons were; my tour as a staff officer had also brought me into close contact with the administration of carriers. When, in December 1943, I completed my tour of duty as Chief of Staff successively to Admirals Tovey and Fraser, I put in for the command of a carrier—and I was given *Victorious*, which was soon to join Task Force 57 where I would serve once again under Admiral Fraser. As Captain of *Victorious*, I took part in all the Pacific operations right up to the end of the war in the home waters of Japan.

At the commencement of World War II the air threat to the United Kingdom was such that His Majesty's Government was rightly spending money on constructing airfields for the RAF, and airfields for the Fleet Air Arm were regarded as of secondary importance. In general, adequate airfields with suitable range and training facilities for the squadrons of the Fleet Air Arm were not available; further, this young and potentially powerful part of the Navy had only been transferred from RAF to RN control in April, 1938. Many experienced RAF officers and men were rapidly withdrawn from the Fleet Air Arm, with consequent weakening of 'air expertise' in the Navy at a time when the Fleet Air Arm was expanding. As a result, the training of Naval Air Squadrons was not nearly good enough. Except in the actual handling of aircraft in the air, the standard of the Naval Air Arm after its expansion was below that of the remainder of the Navy in practically all matters. It was not until the newly formed squadrons left the shore bases and were embarked that the personnel realized the different programmes and duties which became necessary aboard the carrier and which they had not learnt or practised ashore. There is no spare space on a carrier; the ship rolls and pitches; maintenance becomes twice as difficult and to keep a high proportion of the aircraft serviceable requires very careful scheduling.

Whereas it was generally held until 1944 that the efficiency of embarked squadrons depended on the amount of time which could be devoted to training ashore, Admiral Vian commented, it is now the firm opinion of Carrier Commanding Officers that 'the longer the continuous periods the squadrons are embarked and the fewer the interruptions of visits to shore bases the better they become and the more their morale rises. When it becomes practicable to re-establish air groups this point will be met since it is envisaged that groups will be embarked for not less than six months continuously'.

By 1945 the efficiency and gallantry of the carrier-borne Naval Air Squadrons in the Pacific had become fully effective and contributed in a major way to the victory in the Pacific area and to the victorious termination of the war.

Preface

It seems appropriate, at a time when the aircraft carrier may cease to be the main offensive weapon of the Royal Navy and the withdrawal of all British forces from the Far East has been announced, to put on record the achievements of the carriers in reclaiming our Eastern Empire after similar defence economies had brought about their loss. If the men fighting in Burma considered themselves to be the 'Forgotten Army', then surely Task Force 57 has become the 'Forgotten Fleet'. During research for this book I asked an assistant at a famous reference library for information about the British participation in the Okinawa operations and received the reply: 'Okinawa? We didn't do anything there; it was an American show.' Perhaps, after reading this book, he may agree that, although it was perhaps 'an American show', the Royal Navy laid on a brilliant supporting act.

In the writing of this book I am first of all indebted to Admiral of the Fleet Lord Fraser of North Cape, the Commander-in-Chief of Task Force 57, who was kind enough to read and comment on the original draft, and has contributed a foreword; secondly, I am indebted to Admiral Sir Michael Denny, who gave me much first-hand information from his experiences as Captain of *Victorious* and has written the introduction. For the Fleet Air Arm viewpoint I am most grateful to Captain Halliday, D.S.C., Commander Hay, D.S.O., D.S.C., Commander Lamb, D.S.O., D.S.C., and Lieutenant-Commander Pat Chambers, all of whom gave me a lot of their valuable time in the preparation of this book.

I would also like to thank Rear Admiral C. K. Roberts, D.S.O., and Rear Admiral P. N. Buckley, C.B., D.S.O., who started me off on the right lines when I was researching this book, and I must acknowledge also the help of Mr. Edwin Walker, who helped me in some initial research.

For the illustrations, my thanks are due to Admiral Fraser, to the Imperial War Museum, to Commander Donald and to Commander Hay who allowed me to use photographs from his personal collection.

PETER C. SMITH

London,
June, 1969

15

Author's Note

The term 'Task Force' as used throughout this book perhaps needs some explanation. It was originally an American term used to denote a specific assembly of fighting ships gathered together to carry out a particular mission. When they were first so named, these task forces were of a size and composition small enough to be separately identified from a fleet proper. However, as the size and complexity of the United States Navy mushroomed throughout 1943, and the operations carried out grew ever larger and more strategically important, the composition of the task forces also increased until, by 1944, an American task force was approximately the size of any other country's main fleet. By 1945 the US Fleet was made up of four task forces, each of which was worthy of the name 'Fleet' in its own right.

When the British Pacific Fleet was finally formed it represented almost the entire front line strength of the Royal Navy, but—so far had we been outstripped in shipbuilding between 1942 and 1945—even this total strength only approximated to one of the Task Forces of the US Fifth Fleet. The entire British Pacific Fleet, adopting American parlance, was therefore designated Task Force 57.

A further complication arises because the American admirals commanded operations alternately—one would control an operation whilst his opposite number would be planning the next. Whereas the ships largely remained the same, the designation of the fleet would change with its commander. Of the two American admirals with whom this book is mainly concerned, Admiral Spruance commanded the US Fifth Fleet and Admiral Halsey the Third. The BPF also took its number from the over-all American commander and thus it was originally Task Force 57 under Spruance but later served as Task Force 37 under Halsey.

1

Challenge in the East

The fleet which assembled in the Pacific in the summer of 1945, under the command of Admiral Sir Bruce Fraser, was the most powerful and the largest squadron of British and Commonwealth warships to be operated as a single unit during the whole of the Second World War. Acting in conjunction with the United States Fifth Fleet, itself a massive array of naval power, this fleet was designated Task Force 57. It was in fact the full fighting strength of the British Pacific Fleet and, in terms of striking power, represented the strongest force the Royal Navy had assembled up to that time; it existed as a fleet for less than a year, but the reasons for its formation can be traced back for over half a century; the events leading up to its triumphant debut off Okinawa are years signposted with some planning, but with more hesitancy and frustration.

The startling and rapid emergence of Japan as a first-class Imperial power after centuries of almost medieval isolation was not initially fully comprehended in the Western world and there was a widespread under-estimation of their potential, right up to the end of 1941. Then, in December of that year, the United States and Great Britain had their eyes opened in no uncertain manner. It was to take many years, and cost many lives, to recover from the blow which their own blindness had made possible.

The American Admiral Perry's trading expedition of 1853 opened Nipponese eyes to the outside world and, once their leaders had taken the decision to abandon their old way of life, the Japanese quickly and enthusiastically set about closing the two hundred and fifty year gap they had imposed upon themselves. By imitating designs and importing experts from the leading nations of the West—France for her Army and Great Britain for her Navy—

they learned quickly and well. Their insistence on only the best instructors in every field was emphasised by their abrupt dismissal of the French army officers immediately after the Franco-Prussian war and by their replacement with German officers.[1]

Japan's rapid assimilation of modern methods, especially in the military field was quite remarkable and she soon graduated from body armour and spears to machine guns and battleships. The efficiency of the newly-fledged Armed Forces was quickly put to the test; an incident involving a Chinese Naval squadron in 1894 served as a suitable excuse and in the brief war which followed the Chinese were completely and utterly smashed. By this victory Japan gained Korea, Formosa and several Manchurian ports at a single blow. Although dismissed by most European nations as a local squabble and not significant, Russia had taken a knock to her endless designs for expansion—as great under the Czars as they still are under the Soviets.

Always dominating the Russian 'Grand Design' was their need to acquire unrestricted access and control of an ice-free port. To achieve this in the Pacific the seizure of the Chinese harbour of Port Arthur had long been their goal; now the upstart Japanese had taken it. Russia reacted strongly. Persuading France—to whom she was joined by treaty—and Germany—who had territorial aspirations of her own—to join her, Russia presented Japan with a declaration, outwardly with the intention of 'restoring the balance of the Far East', but which in effect, if not in actual wording, told Japan to give up her spoils of war or else . . . Faced by a possible conflict with three of the world's most powerful nations, Japan gave way, with a resulting wave of disillusion and a distrust of Western diplomacy.

This resentment was further increased and given weight when, a few scant years later, under even more doubtful pretexts, these self-same nations, led by Germany, seized various Chinese ports for themselves. It is not surprising then that Japan, still learning, noted these methods and filed her conclusions away for future reference. She had been taught the hard lesson that, beneath the external veneer of polite words and flowery exchanges between nations, the ancient policy of 'Might is Right' still held good in this modern world. Japan would not be caught out again.

[1] It is interesting to speculate on how much of the deep-set rivalry which later so plagued relations between the Japanese Armed Forces stemmed from the ingrained dislike for each other of their former British and German mentors.

The establishment of a large Russian fleet in the Pacific was not only a cause of unease to Japan; Britain, too, had spent many years of effort in curtailing the groping tentacles of the Russian octopus. In the Crimea and on the north-west frontier of India these feelers had been repulsed, but now one had found an outlet; the 'back door' of the Empire had been breached and there were grave fears in Whitehall.

The long established and well tested foreign policy of Great Britain had always been to remain supreme at sea while protecting herself on land with alliances against the most powerful land forces of the period. This policy was tried again but in a modified form. Despite the unending attempts to whittle it down, the Royal Navy at the turn of the century was still the most powerful and most efficient afloat. True, it was no longer a 'Two Power' Navy—it was no longer as strong as its two chief rivals combined—but it retained an absolute and awesome lead over all its established opponents. Gradually this happy state of affairs was threatened and it became increasingly obvious that this comfortable superiority could not be maintained for much longer without greatly increased efforts. With a determined policy for the building up of an Empire as large as that of Great Britain, German's unstable ruler, the Kaiser Wilhelm II, against the advice of Bismarck, had already embarked on a feverish warship building programme, the ultimate aim of which was to achieve equality with Britain in naval tonnage.

Although, by virtue of her long lead and superior ship-building potential, Britain felt able to contain this challenge with a 'Two keels for one' programme of battleship construction, the menacing growth of German military strength and the hostility of that nation's leaders to this country forced Great Britain to concentrate her resources more and more in Home waters. In these circumstances an alliance with Japan was considered opportune in order to hold the Russians in check in Asia, without committing our own resources. A treaty with Japan was accordingly signed in 1902.

Within three short years, the whole balance in the Far East was again upset by the outcome of the Russo-Japanese war of 1904. Increasing friction between the two countries came to a violent head with the Russian occupation of Manchuria and their obvious designs on Korea. With a Russian fleet at least twice the size of their own, the Japanese took the courageous decision that, as they felt unable to ignore this further threat, their only alternative was to wage a quick war in the hope that what they lacked in numbers they could make up with surprise.

They decided to attack and capture Port Arthur. Without awaiting a declaration of war, Japanese destroyers moved against the Russian Pacific Fleet and, in a series of lightning torpedo attacks, sank three Russian battleships. This gave the Japanese army time to invest the Naval Base without opposition from Russian ships. Time was at a premium for the Japanese; the other half of the Russian fleet, based in the Baltic, was being assembled in readiness, and would shortly be despatched to the Pacific via the North Sea and Indian Ocean. Moreover, if it was united with the survivors of the Port Arthur squadron now undergoing repairs, the Japanese would be faced with overwhelming odds and their blockading squadron would be annihilated.

In the event, after a bitter and bloody struggle, the strategic hills overlooking the base were taken and the remaining Russian warships were sunk or disabled at leisure. When the decrepit Baltic Fleet did eventually arrive the following May, after a nightmare voyage around the world, it was met by a refreshed Japanese fleet under Admiral Togo and destroyed. It was a shattering victory for the Japanese, so complete that within the year Russia was forced to come to terms. For Japan, the Treaty of Portsmouth marked a coming of age; for the mighty nations of Europe, absorbed as they were with their own bickerings, it should have been a warning of her increased power but in the tensions of that period this message went largely unheeded.

With the waning of Russian influence, a vacuum was created in the Far East, a vacuum which the Japanese were only too eager to fill. Annexing Korea, they moved on towards total domination of the Chinese mainland. In 1911, the Chinese Republic was formed; this was not at all what the Japanese wanted, as it tended to unite the tottering giant; they became increasingly involved in attempts to overthrow the Republic from the inside hoping thus to create the necessary chaos to provide a smokescreen behind which they could take over those centres of most use to them.

Here, however, Japan received a check, for Britain, although more and more fatally involved with Germany, had not failed to notice that her ally, far from being a stabilising influence in the Far East, had now become the chief cause of unrest. Japan was firmly told to stop interfering in China's affairs. Friendship for

Britain, already on the wane in Japan, now fell to zero; as yet Japan could not challenge her mentor outright, nor ignore her warnings; but she bided her time. Events were moving in favour of Japan.

Once the Great War had got under way, sucking the whole continent into its bloody whirlpool, little thought could be diverted towards Japan's intentions as regards her neighbour. This was the opportunity, and Japan's leaders were well aware of the fact. The only other nation which might have been able to restrain these ambitions was America, but she was still firmly isolationist, although the first hints that she might deviate from this policy were becoming apparent.

The growing confidence of the Japanese in what they considered to be their 'ultimate destiny' was reflected in their 'Twenty-one Demands', presented secretly to China in 1915. These, if conceded, would mean the virtual take-over of every important position in the Chinese administration, and would have reduced that vast country to a mere vassal state. Both the United States and Great Britain got wind of this *diktat*, however, and both made formal protests. These in no way served to deter Japan; it was no longer 1911 and the Japanese government felt no need to pay much attention to either request. Indeed, by the latter part of the war, both nations had tactfully stopped pressing her on those points in return for her co-operation against Germany. In the event Japan although nominally an ally showed very little enthusiasm for the Allied cause, and many Japanese eagerly hoped for a German victory. On Armistice Day it required a curt reminder from her Allies before she joined in the celebrations.

The end of the Great War marked a precise turning point both in history and the distribution of world power. The nations of Europe, after centuries of pre-eminence, were left exhausted and on the brink of a general decline which is still in progress today. On the other hand, the United States was now acknowledged as the richest and most powerful nation on the globe, while Russia in the bloodstained grip of Communism was still embroiled in a cruel civil war. Japan therefore found herself elevated, without any effort on her part, to a position undreamed of fifty years before. In military terms this new standing was firmly consolidated by the Washington Naval Conference and the resulting treaty of 1921. As a direct consequence of this treaty, Japan achieved third rating in tonnage, below that of America and Britain alone.

While Britain toasted the end of the 'war to end all wars', the Japanese did not mean to allow the grass to grow under their feet. They were content after the Washington Treaty to bide their time while Great Britain's strength and influence waned. Their aims had not changed one iota and they merely awaited the next favourable opportunity.

In 1931 heavy pay cuts were applied to the British services resulting in the Invergordon mutiny. All outward appearances seemed to indicate that the Royal Navy was far from its peak as a fighting service and as sea power was the only effective force with which Great Britain could threaten Japan, the Japanese rulers naturally felt their time had come. They were equally contemptuous of the new hope of the world, the much vaunted League of Nations. This hollow edifice was soon revealed for the pompous ineffective sham that it was.

In the autumn of 1931, on the pretext of establishing order after a bomb outrage of doubtful origin, Japan sent a strong force into Manchuria. This army quickly occupied all key points including the capital and with a great fanfare set up a puppet state, solely under Japanese jurisdiction. Against this blatant aggression the League responded with the speed and majesty which has since become the hallmark of such international bodies; they issued a declaration which condemned the Japanese act as illegal and told her to withdraw. Strange as it may have seemed to the League's ardent supporters this dread pronouncement failed to achieve the departure of one Japanese soldier from Manchuria.

The successful aggressor continued to execute her plans unconcerned and the following year a naval landing party was sent ashore in the vicinity of Shanghai. Unfortunately for them the Chinese showed a rare flash of fighting spirit and the invaders were roughly handled. Heavy fighting developed which was only finally brought to a conclusion by the tact and diplomacy of the British Admiral in the area, Sir Howard Kelly, acting unsupported and unthanked. The League made tut-tutting noises and contented itself with that; the British Government was equally unprepared to act. There was certainly no movement of the British Fleet to the Pacific.

The Japanese consolidated their gains and settled down to await their next opportunity. It quickly came; in 1933, Adolf Hitler was elected to power in Germany and led by his Nazi Party this country rapidly rose from a disarmed ineffectual state to the most powerful nation in Europe. Thus the chain of events preceding 1914 were repeated and the Japanese watched gleefully as in quick succession both the reconstructed Germany and Fascist Italy repeated her humiliations of both the League and the Western democracies with their easy conquests of Austria, Abyssinia and Czechoslovakia.

If Great Britain had previously had any ideas of baulking Nipponese ambitions in the Far East in the years 1930–39, then this new turn of events on Britain's European doorstep certainly sent the physical possibility of any effective counter-measure fading into obscurity, as events nearer home became more important. By 1937 the Japanese felt ready for their next move forward. In the summer of that year their armies drove deep into China proper. Their initial gains were large and it was soon apparent that, although the vast size of China would mean a protracted campaign, the Japanese would, in time, be able to control as much of that nation as they desired.

Great Britain could not, or would not, act: what then of the United States?

It was equally in her long-term interests to prevent the establishment of a strong Japanese Empire in South East Asia. Japan had been her potential enemy number one since 1921 although the American fleet was, on paper anyway, greatly superior in size and potential. The deeply ingrained isolationism was slowly being eroded away, but it was still a powerful enough feeling to prevent her leaders, even if they had been so willing, to do more than make warning noises to Tokyo. When it became clear that this type of action was useless, they decided, together with Britain, to apply economic sanctions to persuade Japan peacefully to stop her expansionist policies. As with the sanctions applied against Italy earlier, they made no difference; indeed, they had the direct opposite effect to that required.

Japan was exceedingly vulnerable to most types of sanction which affected her imports and home economy, but above all she was dependent on imported oil. Although far from self-sufficient in most of her major industries, she could to some extent make up for her deficiencies from her conquered territories; with oil, however, this was not possible as almost all of it lay in the control of her likely enemies. As the threat of the ultimate strangulation of the nation grew in size, the ruling martial clique became more and more convinced that the only salvation for Japan as an independent major power lay in a massive gamble. And, after all, 1904 had been a convincing precedent.

When the Western nations finally tightened the economic screw in 1941, the Second World War had already been under way for two years. Japan had been delighted to see prominent European nations go down beneath the tracks of Hitler's Panzers. The lessons made plain to her by Germany's swift victories were that the Western democracies were certainly far less serious opponents than they had up till then believed. Certainly with most of the mother countries under the control of the German Reich—which was friendly to Japan—their former Colonial empires in the Far East lay wide open and very tempting prey. The unhappy Vichy Government was persuaded to allow Japanese expansion southward well before the declaration of war and the Dutch East Indies, with their rich oil fields, were irresistible bait once the sanctions started to bite.

Everything needed for Japan's continued independence lay almost undefended before her and included among these prizes, seemingly ripe for plucking, were the rubber plantations of Malaya and the added bonus of the great Singapore dockyard, recently completed at the expense of the British taxpayer. Thus it can be seen that by building a huge base but not providing basic defences in the form of battleships or aircraft carriers, Britain had in fact constructed an expensive lure rather than a deterrent.

At this stage, 1941, Britain, although down, was not yet out; but to the Japanese, as to most nations at that time, her eventual end seemed inevitable. In any case, fighting for her very existence against both Germany and Italy there would appear to be little she could do to stop a major attack in the East. As a preparation for just this, Japan reached agreement with the Vichy Government for the use of the airfields in Indo-China and she moved her troops up to the Thai border.

Britain noted these movements with concern and, spurred on by the increasingly frantic appeals from Australia and New Zealand, prepared to put into effect the long planned movement of a Battle Fleet eastwards—this despite her preoccupation and heavy losses elsewhere. Unfortunately, the new conception of what constituted the 'Main Fleet' which had so long been promised turned out to be vastly different from what the Commonwealth had come to expect.[1] It finally arrived at Singapore in the shapes of the brand

[1] See Chapter Two, page 35 et seq.

new battleship *Prince of Wales*, the ancient battle-cruiser *Repulse* and four indifferent destroyers. This hotch-potch squadron was greeted with a great fanfare and much jubilation when it sailed into the great new dockyard, but if it was designed to overawe the Japanese it was a case of far too little much too late. Japan was already committed to total war.

The Japanese had decided that the United States Pacific Fleet based at Pearl Harbour was the real danger: the American fleet included eight battleships and two carriers. To eliminate this much more menacing force was a priority target and preparations had already been put in hand to mount a daring surprise raid by carrier based aircraft to deal the Americans a heavy body blow right at the start.

This plan, a combination of the original Port Arthur attack and the more recent British attack on Taranto, was boldly conceived, but side by side with this, further massive air attacks were to be carried out all over Southern Asia to support the swift capture of Singapore, the Philippines, Hong Kong and other Allied bases; these moves would in turn safeguard their thrusts to conquer their ultimate objective, the Dutch East Indies. It proved a masterly plan which worked without a flaw, but was one which was obviously based on a tremendous confidence in their own ability to carry it through.

On that fateful 7th of December when she went to war, Japan carried all before her. At Pearl Harbour the American battle-fleet was smashed and—like a tidal wave—the ships, planes and men of the Rising Sun banner swept their way through the south-western Pacific. Similar to the German blitzkrieg, it seemed that nothing could halt the pell-mell speed with which the Japanese swarmed south. Within a few days of their arrival, the two British capital ships were sunk and not one single heavy ship was left to oppose the Japanese Navy at the start of its offensive. Those Allied warships which remained, a few old cruisers and destroyers, disorganised and outnumbered, with complete air control in their opponents' hands, fought on until sunk in a series of heroic if futile actions. To back up their invasion fleets, the Japanese had ten battleships and the carriers of the Nagumo Task Force to call on if required. But they were not needed; the covering cruiser squadrons sufficed to sweep the area clear.

Had the two British battleships fought off the air attacks of the 10th December, they could not long have survived against such

25

massive odds. One by one the surviving Allied warships were sunk piecemeal or fled ignominiously to Ceylon or Australia. Within three months Malaya, the Philippines, Wake Island, Sumatra, Java, Thailand, Burma, Borneo, all fell. Whole divisions of Imperial troops were sacrificed at Singapore defending that mystical base weeks after the last big ships had left. And before long the Japanese were on Indian soil.

This succession of defeats was watched with mounting alarm in Britain and with horror by the Australians, who saw the long-feared onslaught sweeping even closer while all the old plans and promises for their defence crumbled away before their eyes; there were no longer any illusions to the effect that one Hurricane was worth three Japanese planes. The enemy's alarming expansion was all too similar to the Nazi conquest which had carried the Swastika banner to mastery over most of Europe from the Channel Islands to the Volga River—and there was no sign of a withdrawal.

Although this nation's pre-war policies had contributed largely to this debacle, certain of her current policies were also open to criticism, in particular the amazing—to her Far Eastern subjects—decision to ship convoy after convoy of modern war material to the Soviet Union who had not yet asked for this and certainly never thanked us, instead of reinforcing British forces in the Far East. This aid to Russia was started before the outbreak of the Pacific war, but it would seem clear that the Government was aware of what was building up in the Far East hence the dispatch of the two battleships.[1]

It seemed that the Japanese only had to dare and the whole vast sub-continent of India would fall to them—with overwhelming consequences to the British war effort. It needed little imagination to envisage the German and Japanese members of the Axis linking hands in Persia after their respective thrusts through Egypt, the Ukraine and Burma. There would have been no question of Britain long surviving such a coup, for like Japan her whole

[1] Not only our forces in the Pacific suffered from this slavish support. It is an ironical fact and comment on the Government's sense of priorities that the Naval forces allocated to escort modern war equipment to Murmansk had to use obsolete material to guard it on its journey. Thus Mark I Hurricanes flew from carriers protecting cargo ships carrying Mark III Hurricanes in their holds—a fantastic situation. Witness too the scramble to aid Greece at the expense of probable victory in North Africa in the summer of 1941. Such policies probably had valid reasons to support them, but the fact remains that vital British interests were sacrificed to aid nations that up to then had been very unwilling comrades-in-arms.

effort depended on oil. Loss of the Middle East would have had the same effect on Britain as the total oil embargo would have had on Japan. The final collapse would perhaps have taken a little time, but time was all that it would have taken.

This grim vision was no doubt prominent in the minds of the worried Chiefs of Staff in London and by a frantic feat of assembly a second fleet was somehow mustered and despatched post-haste to the Indian Ocean to anticipate the next Japanese thrust. In view of the critical situation in the Mediterranean, onto which we were only hanging by our finger-nails, it seemed quite an imposing fleet, in numbers at least. But it proved rather a motley collection of warships, with hardly any two ships of the same class —each therefore having differing speeds, ranges, armaments and experience—and most of them considerably over age. Nevertheless, motley or not, it represented every spare warship the Royal Navy could muster. It comprised five battleships, the four remaining 'Royal Sovereigns', all over twenty years old and terribly slow; the equally ancient but modernised *Warspite*; two brand new fleet carriers, *Formidable* and *Indomitable* which, though impressive ships in themselves, were equipped with Sea Hurricane fighters and carried biplanes as their strike aircraft; plus the ancient carrier *Hermes*; some eight cruisers, mainly pre-war types; and about a dozen destroyers of mixed age and condition. This force assembled at Addu Atoll and, under the command of Admiral Somerville, set about practising some rudimentary exercises to enable them to work together.

The force they were preparing to take on consisted of Admiral Nagumo's six big carriers with hundreds of modern and well tried and experienced aircrews together with supporting battle-ships, cruisers and destroyers, which had all been working together as a team for six victorious months. It became quickly obvious to Admiral Somerville that unless he was very careful Britain's second Eastern Fleet would rapidly go the same way as its pre-decessor. Like Admiral Philips before him, however, Somerville had a fleet to defend British territory and therefore had in some way to use it should the threat materialise, otherwise his recently collected warships might just as well disperse to their former war stations now left unguarded. Admiral Somerville came to the conclusion that his only, albeit slim, chance of inflicting enough damage on his opponent and forcing him to withdraw, was by a dusk torpedo attack on the enemy carriers with his antique aircraft. At the same time he had above all to avoid being pin-pointed by his opponent's bombers. He could do nothing else with the force he had available, but stay clear and hope to land a lucky punch from a safe distance. Meantime some more Hurricane fighters had been rushed to Ceylon where, it was hoped, they would be able to prevent Trincomalee being 'Pearl Harboured'.

All these moves were completed only just in time, for on the 23rd March the Japanese occupied the Andaman Islands to the west of Malaya and further movements were clearly indicated. Admiral Somerville decided to meet any enemy thrusts in waters of his own choosing and carried out a cautious probe to the south-east. By April 2nd however no contact had been made and these fruitless wanderings overhung with uncertainty resulted in short-ages among the older vessels of fuel and water, necessitating a return to harbour. The main force therefore again put into Addu Atoll but the *Hermes* was detached to Trincomalee to restore while the cruisers *Dorsetshire* and *Cornwall* were sent to Colombo to effect long-needed repairs.

It was at this juncture that a sighting report came in informing Somerville that the Japanese Task Force had been sighted 350 miles south-east of Ceylon. Seldom has any commander been caught on the wrong foot so completely. At once the 'fast' divi-sion of the fleet sailed again, leaving the 'Royal Sovereigns' to catch up as best they could. But once again all further attempts to make contact proved fruitless although it is a moot point as to whether this was entirely unfortunate as the enemy soon demon-strated his efficiency.

Scout planes from the enemy carriers located the two unescor-ted heavy cruisers heading back to the fleet from Colombo and within a very short time they were pounced on by a horde of bombers and sunk. Next the Japanese struck at Colombo itself hoping to find the British Fleet there—the base at Addu Atoll was unknown to them. They inflicted serious damage to installations there and then withdrew. The strength of the enemy strikes had shown Somerville that it was unwise to divide his meagre strength and he fell back to regroup with the 'slow' division of his force. The Admiralty appeared to have a bad attack of nerves when it was learnt that a second enemy Task Force was active in the Bay of Bengal; Somerville's fleet seemed to be in grave danger and they advised him to fall back to East Africa if hard pressed.

Having failed to locate the British main fleet on the 7th and

8th the Japanese decided to hit Trincomalee in the hope of finding some worthwhile targets there and in this they were successful. On the approach of the bombers the old *Hermes* was ordered to sea and no air cover materialized; she was discovered by the jubilant Nipponese airmen. Both she and her lone destroyer escort went down under a veritable rain of bombs; never before had such a great percentage of hits and near misses been obtained.

On concluding this object lesson on the correct use of modern naval power the Japanese then withdrew. At the time, April 1942, this withdrawal, made before Somerville's fleet was finished off, seemed inexplicable, but the enemy fleet was required in the Pacific to fulfil the latest objects in the Japanese Grand Strategy; and so the British were granted a reprieve. Far from being a forerunner of further Japanese expansion westward, this raid had been made solely to keep the Royal Navy quiet while their true targets, Midway Island and New Guinea, were occupied.

In the pursuit of these twin objectives the Japanese received their first checks. The Americans now took a hand. First the Japanese failed to win the Battle of the Coral Sea in May. Then, a month later, the grandiose invasion of Midway was shattered by the crews of the US Navy's Dauntless dive-bombers. After these two setbacks came the murderous eye-to-eye slogging match at Guadalcanal in the Solomons. When this campaign was finally concluded in February 1943 the Japanese found themselves very much on the defensive.

In the meantime the British fleet in the Indian Ocean was gradually run down as its ships were required for more active zones of war, and by 1943 it had virtually ceased to exist. It was therefore left to the United States Navy to beat the Japanese at their own game.

Even before the Pacific war had opened, Japan's most famous sailor, Admiral Yamamoto, had warned his countrymen that, should war come, the Navy would run wild for six months, but should hostilities continue beyond this period he could foresee little hope of ultimate victory. His predictions proved remarkably accurate. Japan had gained the initial advantages of all aggressor states, in particular surprise combined with superior fighting equipment, and the Allies, with their confused and outdated systems of defence, had indeed allowed her to achieve victory after victory.

It was only to be expected, however, that once America, the

greatest industrial nation of the world, geared her home economy to the war effort, the inevitable attrition suffered in battle would be to her long-term advantage. With her factories and dockyards completely secure from reprisal, she was able within a very brief period, by the wise adoption of new methods and weapons on a grand scale, to create a brand new fleet of awe-inspiring size and complexity, armed with all the most sophisticated equipment of the time.

By contrast Japan's forces were a compact élite; with each major battle more and more of her incomparable veterans fell never to be replaced. Her crack air squadrons and ships were destroyed and she could only replace them at a fraction of the speed which could be maintained by the vast American resources. Her only hope of victory would have been by inflicting upon the Americans a further series of slashing defeats before they had time to recover from their initial pounding. Ship for ship, the Japanese were still, in the summer of 1942, more than a match for the untried Americans, but instead of grasping their opportunity the Japanese allowed their resources to be dissipated in scores of violent but minor actions in which, although they often came out victorious, they never succeeded in annihilating their opponent's main fleet.

2

Inquest on Disaster

The Washington Treaty of 1921 formed the blueprint on which all subsequent developments with regard to the Royal Navy's strength were based. It was unfortunate that this treaty tended to deal more in actual numbers of warships rather than in national commitments, for it proved to be a terrible handicap to all subsequent British Naval planning.

In the early twenties, then, having reduced her own naval power to an alltime low, Great Britain had to face the unpalatable fact that the most likely potential enemy at sea in any future war would be that self-same Japan whom they had so recently assisted to such eminence. This posed many difficult questions to the planners at the Admiralty: to match the new Japanese Fleet, ship for ship, at least two-thirds of the reduced strength of the Royal Navy would need to be either based in, or despatched to, the Far East, a somewhat disturbing thought to both the Admiralty and the British taxpayer alike. Secondly, if the occasion did arise, then where was such a huge force to be based? The obvious choice was Australia; a fully developed harbour was available at Sydney and, moreover, it was secure. Australia was staunchly pro-British and would obviously welcome such massive defences against the menace of Japanese expansion. This option was considered but not chosen. Instead, it was decided to create an entirely new base and dockyard from virgin jungle at Singapore Island. It appears that the main factor which caused this decision was that Singapore was considered to be better placed both as a defensive base to cover India and as a jumping-off base to protect Australia. Sydney would have been a cheaper choice and was more readily available, but its position, although facing the Pacific, was not ideal because it was so far from Japan.

Another reason for the abandonment of Sydney as a major base for the Royal Navy has been suggested. This was that the Admiralty was reluctant to despatch the major portion of the Navy for an unknown period to Australian waters, far from their immediate control.[1] Whether this theory can be seriously accepted is open to question. In any case, with the firm decision taken to build up Singapore, any other alternatives were dropped.

It is interesting to note that almost at once the new base itself became the focal point in the planners' minds, rather than the ships which were to operate from it. This preoccupation with what was in reality purely a supporting project rather than with the basic priorities has occurred quite frequently in British defence planning: an increasing involvement with some large-scale undertaking such as a fixed base gradually obscures the main issue to which it should be subordinate. Here we are considering the Singapore base, but this inability to concentrate the main effort on to the essentials can be illustrated from more recent events: the building up of a base in Suez, its abandonment, followed by the development of a new base in Cyprus, only for that also to be abandoned, is an obvious example; the same misguided thinking can be seen over Aden and, more recently, over Bahrein. The development of the base at Singapore became almost an obsession with the defence planners, politicians and the public alike. Over the years this grew into an unconscious feeling that the *base itself* would provide our defence against the Japanese navy. Glowing details were revealed about the great 15-inch guns mounted to protect the sea approaches to the island, and these were seized on by the press as symbols of its impregnability. What was forgotten was that, unlike the equivalent 15-inch guns carried by the Royal Navy's fast dwindling numbers of battleships, guns which were as mobile as their parent vessels, the guns on Singapore Island were static defences. In the event, the attack on Singapore developed from the landward side of the island and they were therefore powerless to play any part at all. Even if a direct amphibious assault on the island itself had been mounted from the sea, the entire Japanese fleet was not very likely to steam conveniently into range and offer itself up for destruction—but nothing less could really vindicate these immobile monsters, powerless to follow an enemy who could withdraw and outflank at will. Not so our battleships, but this basic fact was overlooked in the general adulation of something *new*; battleships were old hat, no longer necessary. In fact, in the

---

[1] See *Main Fleet to Singapore* by Russell Grenfell (Faber).

HMS *Victorious*   [*Commander Hay*

Top:
Avenger

Commander Hay]

Centre:
Firefly

*Imperial
War Museum]*

Bottom:
Hellcat

Commander Hay]

twenties and thirties when the base was planned, it still needed battleships to sink battleships, but this point was not considered relevant to determined policy. Instead the small number of these ships we still possessed was steadily reduced, while the base from which they would operate gained in status as an alternative.

In the event the actual construction of the Singapore base was proceeded with only slowly for in common with every other facet of national defence in that halcyon period it became a political shuttlecock, used together with the 'Bomber versus Battleship' controversy as an excuse for making no decisions at all. Successive governments came and went, mouthing the same platitudes of 'Collective Security' and pious references to the League of Nations.

With money in short supply, the work dragged on and on. As long as the dockyard itself was still not completed, the Admiralty had a valid reason for not actually despatching a squadron of the expected Pacific Fleet eastwards. The Royal Navy remained concentrated in home waters and the Mediterranean where they alternated from cruises around the European ports to tactical exercises based on variations on the Battle of Jutland.

Again, exactly why these fleets were in training so near home is difficult to say. France was friendly. The only other European power with a large navy at all in 1930 was Italy and she too remained passive until the mid-thirties; in any case her traditional argument was with France. Only Japan appeared actively hostile and where our ships and crews ought to have been training was in the waters of the Pacific and Indian Oceans. Scattered over this vast area, the Royal Navy only maintained a few slender forces, consisting usually of an aircraft carrier, a cruiser squadron with a few destroyers, submarines and small auxiliaries.

When the Australian and New Zealand Governments, and our numerous commercial interests in Malaya, Borneo, Burma and India, required reassurance, it became a standard reply to state that in the event of possible conflict with Japan the 'Main Fleet' would be despatched to Singapore. This reply developed over the years into an understanding, if nothing more, that if war should threaten practically the whole Royal Navy would be on the scene to protect them within a very short time. By 1940, it was accepted that the Royal Navy would arrive within seventy days.

Exactly what practical preparations were made for this massive redeployment is difficult to ascertain. A vast amount of organisation of the highest order would be required both to dispatch such a force and to maintain it throughout a protracted campaign so far from Britain with no major base yet ready to support it.

If training for Pacific warfare was essential, but not in fact carried out on a large enough scale, then of equal importance certainly was warship design. A warship has necessarily to cram within confined limitations everything needed to be able to present the maximum offensive and defensive power towards the enemy. British warships are often said to be built so that they are capable of operating anywhere in the world with the same degree of efficiency. While that may have been true in the days of sail, the introduction of steam had radically changed this concept. Prior to the First World War the bulk of the British warships laid down were designed primarily for a conflict with Germany. The battleships, light cruisers and destroyers completed during the years 1910–20 were all designed to defeat the opposing German vessels of the Kaiser's Navy. This of course was right and proper policy at a time of major conflict and in the normal course of events these ships would have been phased out and replaced by new construction—which would naturally have been designed with the possibility of Pacific warfare in mind.

Unfortunately for the Navy—and ultimately for all British subjects in Asia in 1942—having already been crippled in its defensive capabilities by wholesale scrapping, the Navy was further handicapped by the disastrous 'Ten Year Ruling'. This came into effect in 1923 and, as it stood, although bad enough, could be justified; what was not initially revealed was that it contained a 'receding' clause. Basically, it was founded on the assumption that there would not be a major war for ten years, which was fair enough in 1923, though risky; but instead of the replacement of obsolete tonnage being allowed to commence in 1933, each year that passed saw a further extension of the ten years, so that in effect the decade of standstill rolled on and on into the future.

And so, on the outbreak of war in 1939, the most modern battleships in the Royal Navy were the *Nelson* and *Rodney*, completed no less than twelve years before. All the others—including the *Hood* which went into commission in 1920—had either been completed during the Great War, or had been designed for that war. Exactly how ships built to operate in the North Sea, just a few hours steaming from their home bases, were supposed to take part in a successful war against Japan across the vast stretches of the Pacific was a question few of our leaders cared to ask—even supposing it crossed their minds. Indeed, the very scale of distances in the Pacific is daunting; from Singapore to Tokyo is over 2,500 miles and from Japan to the nearest Commonwealth harbour, Sydney, is 4,400 miles.

Over the previous century the Royal Navy had built up a widespread chain of small bases all over the globe so that our distant squadrons could operate anywhere in the world in the sure knowledge that supplies would be readily available. With the change over to coal in the latter part of the nineteenth century no change of policy was envisaged. Indeed why should it be—the existing bases were all secure and provision was made to hold stocks of coal fuel at them. When oil came into general use provisions for refuelling followed the same pattern. A mobile fuelling force as an alternative was not really necessary and was liable to be enormously expensive. As we have seen, the Navy was hard pressed to provide even the minimum numbers of warships, let alone to take on additional programmes of auxiliary vessels for afloat support. The actual idea of anything resembling a fleet train was not extensively considered until 1937 and then it was the threat of heavy bombing on established bases in Europe and the Mediterranean which was the main consideration and not the inherent advantages of a mobile base.

Therefore the Admiralty was confronted with a complex list of hypothetical problems, if and when the actual clash came; if they appear to have found the solution to very few of them, then it can only be repeated that the basic root of their failure was due to no small extent to the vacillations and short-sighted policies of successive inter-war governments with their crippling financial cuts in defence.

In 1930 it had been agreed that some obsolete tonnage in the world's battleship forces could be replaced, providing the previously agreed ratios in total tonnage were observed. But that same year the British Government—in the face of no very strenuous opposition from their opponents in the House—became further embroiled with the London Naval Treaty. This resulted in the abandonment of any replacement of Naval tonnage in battleships for a further six years and is the reason why the 'Queen Elizabeth' and 'Royal Sovereign' classes still formed the bulk of the fleet in 1939. Worse still, from the British point of view, was an agreement to limit total cruiser and destroyer tonnages.

For this country, utterly dependent as she is on seaborne supplies, this was a crippling blow. Neither Japan nor America needed to use their destroyers for convoy duties as we did; the majority of their ships were available for fleet duties. Britain on the other hand had learnt—at terrible cost—that scores of these vessels were needed to protect our merchantmen in time of war: near mass-starvation in 1917 was only averted by the switching of the bulk of our destroyer strength to convoy work. Therefore, to accept parity with other nations in destroyer tonnages might appear on paper to be fair and equal, and to the casual reader of *Jane's Fighting Ships* did appear so, but in reality such a pledge was a noose around our necks. The critical shortage of flotilla vessels throughout the Second World War stems from this suicidal policy of intellectual reason.

It was not until 1937, following the general resumption of warship construction after a fifteen-year break, that Britain planned to replace its fifteen old battleships with a well balanced force centred on the five battleships of the 'King George V' class—which conformed to the old treaty limitations of 35,000 tons—and four, later five, of the larger 'Lion' class battleships of 40,000 tons. The tonnage of these latter was increased over the imposed limitations when it was learnt that the Germans were building the 42,000-ton *Bismarck* and *Tirpitz*.[1]

In addition to the battleships, a force of seven modern carriers was planned, of which the first, *Ark Royal*, was to be followed by six of the improved and armoured 'Illustrious' type. From the Admiralty plans to replace her fifteen outdated battleships with a modern force of ten battleships and seven carriers, it can be seen that the Admiralty was not so anti-air-minded as we have sometimes been led to believe.

This well-balanced programme was soon drastically altered, for the German U-boats' unrestricted campaign of slaughter against our merchant shipping soon focused attention on the lack of flotilla vessels brought about by the London Treaty. Britain did not have the resources to build up her destroyer and escort strength

[1] Our ships can be compared with the projected German 54,000-tonners and Japan's *Yamato* rating 76,000 tons. Like Britain, both Italy and France stuck to the 35,000-ton limit, but the Americans went for 45,000 tons with the 'Iowas' and Germany had wild dreams of 144,000-ton monsters with 20.5 inch guns which gives some indication on how they felt towards the treaties by which we felt absolutely bound.

as well as her main battle fleet, so necessity forced the complete abandonment of the 'Lion' class and delayed the completion of two of the 'King George V's' and two of the 'Illustrious' carriers.

This cut-back—added to the heavy losses sustained by the Royal Navy in 1941, when the *Barham, Hood* and *Ark Royal* were sunk, and the *Queen Elizabeth, Valiant, Formidable* and *Illustrious* were put out of action for months with heavy damage—left the Admiralty so denuded of ships that no more than a token force could be detached to the Pacific.

A final decision was made, under Winston Churchill's influence, to send a small, highly mobile force which, it was hoped, would form the best deterrent. The brand new *Prince of Wales*, the old but fairly fast *Repulse*, the new carrier *Indomitable* and six modern destroyers were selected for the task. Almost at once even this much reduced fleet was further cut down. While working up in the West Indies the *Indomitable* ran aground and was damaged; there were no other modern carriers available as *Victorious* was needed for the Home Fleet. And two years of warfare had shown that aircraft carriers were essential in a modern fleet. In fact the *Hermes* was in the Indian ocean, and thus available, but she was small, slow and old and had been sent there more for her own protection than for anything else; she was certainly not suitable to be pitted against torpedo or dive-bomber forces, or against modern battleships—the fate of the *Glorious* had amply proved this. The lack of reliable air support was later to prove fatal. To make matters worse, instead of the six modern destroyers promised, all that could eventually be spared were four fairly recent ships, two of which were suffering from defects. Any additional cruisers and destroyers would have to come from the obsolete vessels relegated to the Eastern areas during 1940–41. A far cry this from the long awaited 'Main Fleet'.

The Japanese were not impressed and went ahead as planned. What justification did they have in assuming their absolute ascendancy over the two major Western powers—two countries who held a very low opinion of the fighting capabilities and equipment of their oriental opponent?

It cannot be denied that the Allies were complacent. All the pointers to Japan's strength and ability had been largely ignored, although this can be accounted for to some extent by the deliberate Japanese policy of concealing their strength and flaunting

their weaknesses. Modern Japanese warships rarely showed themselves to Western eyes; instead their most ancient ships showed
the flag the world over. To the rival navies, the Japanese fleet
was made to look a laughing stock. It was a simple deception—and
it worked.

In many facets of sea warfare, and in particular air/sea warfare,
Japan had nothing at all to learn either in design or application
of hardware. Their navy had been subjected to the same treaties
as ours, but, disregarding capital ships for the moment, they had
the advantage of the fact, that, even keeping within their treaty
ratio, they could build their fleet up with new ships whereas the
Royal Navy had to reduce their numbers by scrapping. The
Japanese could therefore implement new ideas more readily than
we could.

The Japanese heavy cruisers produced in the early thirties were
far more workmanlike ships than our barn door 'Counties';
they carried a much heavier armament and were more heavily
protected. And then the Japanese navy was not exactly scrupulous
with regard to the precise displacements allowed under the treaty.
Ship for ship, their cruisers undoubtedly showed far more apprecia-
tion of modern conditions.

The Japanese destroyer flotillas were over a decade in advance
of British ships built in the same period. By 1930 their ships were
carrying six dual-purpose 5-inch guns in weather-proof turrets,
while British destroyers laid down as late as 1940 were designed
to carry four single low-angled guns in open shields. The Japanese
ships were designed naturally exclusively for the Pacific: their
radius of action was good and they were much larger and generally
faster than the British. In addition, by the outbreak of war, they
were armed with the *Long Lance* torpedo, a devastating ship-to-
ship weapon. A comparison of the *Long Lance* with its Allied equivalents makes revealing reading:

	Speed in Knots	*Range in Metres*	*Charge in Kilos*
Great Britain	46	3,000	320
	30	10,000	320
United States	48	4,000	300
	32	8,000	300
Japan	49	22,000	500
	36	40,000	500

Then there were the Japanese capital ships. Japan had withdrawn from all treaty obligations in 1934, which had given them

a three year lead; it was expected that Japan's new battleships would somewhat outclass our own, but what no one dreamed of was the result. Armed with 18-inch guns and virtually unsinkable by gunfire, both *Yamato* and *Musashi* took enormous punishment before they were finally disposed of.

What mattered even more, because of the way the Pacific war developed, was the fact that the Japanese navy was the most advanced in the use of naval aviation. The fact that their battleship force had been frozen at sixty per cent of the Allies had given them an added spur to develop an alternative. Between the wars their Fleet Air Arm rapidly increased in skill and material. It was far more efficient, for example, than its Army counterpart, and the war in China enabled detailed testing to be carried out in combat conditions. By far the most successful aircraft in its day was the Zeke, or Zero, fighter, developed by the Japanese navy. It was a cannon and machine gunned interceptor with a speed of well over three hundred miles an hour; it was also highly manoeuvrable. Compare it with the main land-based fighter available to the defenders of Malaya, the American-built Brewster Buffalo; this was announced as the most advanced fighter aircraft in the Pacific and was originally designed as a carrier interceptor. It did have an equivalent top speed to the Zeke, but was completely outclassed in manoeuvrability and firepower. The front line fighter of the Royal Navy at this period was the Fairey Fulmar, a clumsy two-seater plane with a top speed of only two hundred and sixty miles an hour. It had no cannon and was armed with machine guns only.

The Japanese navy's torpedo and dive-bomber squadrons were highly trained and skilled in anti-shipping techniques. A combination of these two forms of attack had been long proven the most effective way of sinking any vessel from a battleship down, but only the Japanese and Americans had become fully efficient at its massed execution. The Royal Navy had in 1940 demonstrated to the world the effectiveness of even second-rate naval aviation. By sinking the German light cruiser *Konigsberg* off Norway in a brilliantly performed dive-bombing attack it had proved the superiority of this method of warship-busting over the RAF's method of altitude bombing. The subsequent comparisons between the repeated successes of the German Stukas as opposed to the failure of the British Wellingtons and Italian Savoias against ship targets had firmly driven this lesson home. Nevertheless, after their initial success at Bergen, all dive-bombers were withdrawn from the Navy and were never used by the RAF who continued to talk of them as failures even after the battle for Crete had shown their power.

Again, the Taranto attack had shown what an important weapon the torpedo-bomber had become, but again the Royal Navy's main aerial striking forces throughout 1941–42 still consisted of obsolete Swordfish and Albacore biplanes, with top speeds of well under two hundred miles an hour and torpedoes carried externally.

The Japanese navy's Kate was a sleek monoplane and although it also carried its load of torpedoes externally it could do so at speeds of two hundred and thirty miles an hour. The lack of suitable British Naval aircraft was in the main due to the period of 'dual control' when, from 1918 until 1937, all carrier-based aircraft were under RAF control and were treated as a very poor relation when it came to the allocation of the limited funds available. So much for hardware, with the Japanese winning on points everywhere.

But the Japanese were to gain one more unexpected advantage: in spite of our considerable knowledge of their intentions, they managed to achieve surprise. The shock achieved by their attack on Pearl Harbour in 1941 is all the more amazing when one compares it with the opening of the Russo-Japanese war in February 1904. The parallels were there for all to see. Japan felt threatened in 1941 by the introduction of the oil embargo; she had felt the same in 1904 when confronted by Russian expansion. Any nation worthy of its name, faced with a choice between slow strangulation or a fighting chance, invariably chooses the latter. In 1941 the Japanese airmen found the American aircraft lined up in neat rows on their runways; in 1904 their sailors had found the Russian fleet at anchor *outside* Port Arthur, with lights ablaze and guns unmanned. This, despite the fact that in both instances peace negotiations had been abruptly broken off some hours beforehand.

All these factors contributed to the success of the initial Japanese thrusts. However, the very nature of their first massive defeats gave the Americans the clue as to how to reorganise their shattered defences. By destroying half the American battle fleet at Pearl Harbour, Japan had left her opponent no choice but to fight back with all that remained—her aircraft carriers.

Battleships were still to play an important part in the Pacific war and the United States completed no less than ten new ships of this type up till 1945; but theirs was no longer the dominant role. Sea/air power was the key to Japanese conquest and so it was to be instrumental in her ultimate downfall.

Unlike the British, the Americans were quick to learn from their initial mistakes and they had the resources to quickly put the lessons into practice on a large scale.[1] Only in their continued use of wooden flight decks for their carrier fleet did the Americans show a puzzling lack of understanding.

To protect their orthodox warships from the now proven deadly combination of torpedo and dive-bomber assault, large numbers of carriers were necessary and over twenty of the big 'Essex' class were ordered. To supplement these, so pressing was the need for carrier-borne aircraft, numerous fast oilers and light cruisers were completed from the hull up as light fleet carriers, while to provide continual air cover over beach-heads a cheaper slower version was introduced using a mercantile hull, although later classes were built as carriers throughout. These vessels were capable of being mass produced. They were termed 'escort carriers' because of the useful work they did on the Atlantic convoy routes when numerous ships of this type were handed over to the Royal Navy under the Lease-Lend Agreement. The first actual escort-carrier, the *Audacity*, had in fact been British, but again we failed to follow this original idea up and only subsequently built six others of the type. Again initially we flew old Swordfish types from ours, whereas the Americans were more fortunate. Their aircraft, although of a more suitable standard than ours, had been shown to be outclassed by the main Japanese types. Even their most modern fighter, the Wildcat, was not good enough, so they at once set to work to design a naval fighter for their new carrier fleet which would combine all the Zeke's best qualities plus a bit extra. Very soon large swarms of this new interceptor, the Hellcat, began to dominate the air over the Pacific and the Japanese had no immediate reply.

Just coming into service with the US Navy in 1942 was the new Avenger torpedo-bomber and, although it made a tragic debut

---

[1] This lack of defending aircraft and anti-aircraft capacity resulted in ships being pitted against dive-bombers long after it was shown to be fatal. Thus with Norway and Dunkirk a year behind them, Cunningham's fleet sustained heavy losses in the same manner off Crete; yet again, a year later, three out of four patrolling British destroyers were lost in the same manner; even in 1943 ships were being sent in to the Aegean—which was surrounded by German bomber bases—unescorted by fighters.

at the Battle of Midway, it soon proved itself to be the best of its type built for any navy—compare its workmanlike lines and sturdy construction with the clumsy Barracuda produced for the Royal Navy a year later. Avengers soon replaced these sad efforts aboard British carriers, although our navy tended to use their version as dive-bombers and anti-submarine aircraft rather than in its designed role. It certainly performed ably in these roles but it was a basic misuse of the aircraft.

The US Navy's standard dive-bomber, the Dauntless, was a well designed aircraft and, although later superseded by the new Helldiver, did more than any other plane to change the course of the Pacific war.

In addition to the airborne side of offence and defence the Americans developed their anti-aircraft defences using light automatic weapons in heavy concentrations, in particular employing the 40-mm Bofors gun. When these were mounted in batches of eighty to a hundred in battleships, forty on cruisers and ten on destroyers, they provided a deadly-effective shield of fire. The Bofors weapon had been available to the Royal Navy before the war but had been rejected in favour of an improved pom-pom and light .5-inch machine guns. Once the Luftwaffe got to work, the Bofors was quickly put into production, but the delay was to cost us dear in ships and men; and we could never produce them in sufficient quantities to provide our ships with more than a fraction of the American fleet's firepower—which by 1945 was greater than the whole anti-aircraft defences of the British Isles. One British invention which did have a marked effect on barrage fire was the close-proximity fuse; it was used to the mutual advantage of both the Allied fleets and much increased the effectiveness of a ship's fire against air targets.

Starting afresh, the Americans called in civilian consultants to advise them on how to standardise as much equipment as possible to allow quicker replacement. This policy reaped dividends. Standardisation of the twin 5-inch gun as the major secondary armament on all big ships, and as the main armament of destroyers and such, was a typical example. By contrast, the Royal Navy had no less than five different calibres of varying marks to perform the same functions.

From all this it could be foreseen that by mid-1943 the American Navy would be strong enough to go over to the offensive, but in the meantime the Japanese had to be held with what was available—or else Australia would fall. This could not be done by sitting still and allowing the Japanese to establish themselves on their outer perimeter of defences without interference.

The problem was made easier for the Allies by the wave of over-confidence which began to cloud Japanese judgement. In every operation up to the fall of the Dutch East Indies and their raid into the Indian Ocean they had always allowed themselves an ample margin of superiority at each vital point, thus always ensuring ultimate victory. For their attempt to secure the whole of New Guinea they allowed themselves, for the first time, to be matched. And here they received their first major check.

The Battle of the Coral Sea was the first solely carrier-to-carrier battle of the war, but in its small way it set the pattern for all the subsequent actions. The results showed that luck, the weather and strong nerves were of equal importance to firepower, and although the battle could be termed a tactical win for the Japanese, they were frustrated in their plan to capture Port Moresby. The taking of the port was vital to the over-all Japanese plan to conquer New Guinea and their failure at once relieved the pressure on Australia.

This was the first setback for the Japanese; its significance could perhaps be glossed over. The second reverse was more conclusive, because this time the Japanese did not repeat their mistake of applying insufficient force. The invasion of tiny Midway Island in June 1942 was a huge operation, planned and executed with overwhelming strength on the Japanese side; this time they had sufficient force, but they allowed a dispersal of their efforts by complicating the plan with a totally unnecessary attack on the Aleutian Islands. Despite their over two to one supremacy in carriers, they were not only thwarted in their designs, but received a terrible beating and suffered heavy losses, especially to their irreplaceable aircrews. Complete mismanagement of their large battleship force also helped to bring about their defeat; by keeping these powerful ships well back in the field they rendered them powerless to intervene in any way. Had they have been thrust several hundred miles ahead of the main carrier fleet, with the Aleutians-bound carriers with them, the Americans would have been faced with the unpleasant choice of against which force to direct their attacks. Had the Americans still concentrated, as they did, on the Japanese carriers, they would then have run a very grave risk of having their lightly escorted ships annihilated by the enemy battleship force. The Americans had nothing bigger than heavy cruisers at Midway. If the Americans had taken the other course, then the Japanese invasion force might well have succeeded, while the battleships slogged it out at sea. As it was all the Japanese losses achieved nothing and the United States received a much needed boost in morale at a critical moment.

The grim, dour struggle in the Solomon Islands saw the attrition which the Japanese had feared start to take its toll. Despite some brilliant naval victories the end result was that when the last Japanese soldier was evacuated from Guadalcanal in February 1943, the Imperial Navy had apparently lost its sense of drive and purpose; it was forced more and more to adopt a defensive role which was totally alien to it. The Japanese military man had always been taught that the offensive was the ultimate role of every man and while this was possible the Japanese had fought with a fanatical skill and a great disregard for personal safety. Once the tide had turned they found the greatest difficulty in readapting and thus every defensive battle brought forth its 'Banzai' charge against the American troops who were unable to comprehend this apparent will to self-destruction in their opponent. Ultimately this basic urge to sacrifice everything to attack led to the introduction of the Kamikazes, a final defiant gesture against the sweeping tide of Allied victory.

By contrast the United States Navy was beginning to flex its new-found muscles with increasing confidence and this continued to be the story throughout 1943. As island after island fell and the Allies gradually fought closer to Japanese headquarters in Rabaul, the main bulk of the Japanese fleet remained passive and inactive. It offered no challenge to the new American Task Forces which were steadily growing in size and power. By the end of the year these Task Forces were striking hard at the island chains forming the Japanese outer defences of their 'co-prosperity sphere', the Carolines and the Marianas.

Early the following year the Americans felt strong enough to launch their first major offensive, developing the strategy of leap-frogging from base to base and leaving others isolated in their rear to be mopped up later.

The objective chosen for the first major American assault was the island of Saipan, the key base of the Marianas group. This was known to have been heavily fortified and had been reinforced with aircraft and troops. The Japanese plan in the event of invasion was to use this large concentration of aircraft in conjunction with their main fleet and thus deliver a crushing blow to any attacker. It is interesting to note here that the landbased aircraft were composed almost entirely of Naval squadrons: Army-Navy co-operation was sadly lacking on the Japanese side.

Against these defences the United States prepared to throw her main fleet, by now consisting of no less than fifteen carriers with massive numbers of supporting ships; to soften up the islands' defence system there was a huge bombarding fleet centred around her old pre-war battleships of which she still had an imposing number. To back up all this, and also to support the assault groups and troops, the Americans had by this time built up an impressive floating support system. Building up from scratch, they had constructed on mercantile-type hulls, specialist ships for every purpose, Ammunition Ships, Supply Vessels, Aircraft Transports, Repair Ships and Oilers, in fact everything needed to keep her huge fleet at an almost constant peak effectiveness many hundreds of miles from their nearest harbours or anchorages. Every one of these vessels was manned and commissioned as a fighting ship with Naval crews, thus ensuring a uniformly high standard of skill and co-operation.

In June 1944 this Armada struck Saipan and the neighbouring islands causing massive damage to shore installations. All the Japanese attempts at counter blows were thwarted by the US fleet's fighter and gun defences and very soon all the aircraft flown in to the islands earlier had been used up without affecting the American Task Forces at all.

The Japanese had been caught off guard by the early date of the attack and her main fleet was not yet fully prepared to go to the island's aid. When they did finally arrive, they found no shore-based planes fit enough to act with them; even so, with nine carriers, which is more than they had ever used together before, the Japanese felt confident of repelling the assault and inflicting heavy damage on their enemy. In fact, the resulting Battle of the Philippine Sea turned out to be the greatest single defeat yet suffered by the Japanese Navy.

The huge air fleet the Japanese sent against the American Task Forces was met en route to their targets by every interceptor the Americans could get into the air and it was decimated. The few Japanese bombers that did survive were cut to pieces by the weight

47

of the fleet's fire and inflicted very little damage to any American unit.

In the meantime US submarines had sunk two of the Japanese carriers. But even this made little difference, as the Japanese had only enough aircraft left to fill one. When the counter strikes of Avengers and Helldivers found the remainder of the fleet the next day they were for all intents and purposes unopposed in the air. The shattered remnants of the enemy fleet limped back to their bases, while the occupation of the Marianas went ahead. This operation marked the beginning of the end for Japan. In fact she was beaten. But she would not admit it and she carried on for another year. A frantic training scheme was started to rebuild yet again her air power, but there was no longer sufficient time left. The ball was in the US Navy's court, and they were soon on the move again.

The Japanese decided that against the next attack they would throw all their remaining naval strength, regardless of loss, in the remote hope that they could inflict enough damage on their opponent to persuade him to come to a favourable peace. Last ditch sorties were all that remained open to them now, but they still had a powerful surface fleet and could still hit hard . . .

As the Americans in the Pacific gathered their resources to strike hard at the crumbling but still formidable outer defences of the Japanese Empire, it was clear that a great deal of titanic effort and sacrifice would still be required before victory could be achieved. Although now on the defensive the enemy had proved fanatically courageous and it was therefore clear that the defeat of Japan would not be cheaply bought.

Meanwhile the whole Japanese flank lay open on the areas bordering the Indian Ocean. Here was an ideal opportunity for the British, long predominant in that region, to strike from behind the main fronts and contribute to the final great offensives, but in 1943 no such move was made. The reasons for this are clear. Although willing and indeed eager to make such an effort, the task was simply far beyond the resources of this country, fully committed in the Mediterranean and on the home front as she was.

We must therefore retrace our steps in order to clarify the dilemma the British found themselves in during 1942.

3

Rebuilding a Fleet

Even in the darkest days of 1942, when our forces were retreating on all fronts, it was the determined policy of the War Cabinet that, when possible, Great Britain would return in force to the Far East, in company with her Australian and American allies. It proved impossible for Britain to accomplish this as quickly as she would have wished due to the acceptance of Germany as the major enemy; this naturally entailed the concentration of the bulk of the available British Naval strength in European waters. The essential operations which had to be completed before Britain could again turn eastward fell into three broad categories.

Firstly—if Britain was to survive at all—the basic requirement was, as it had always been, to keep the main North Atlantic sea route open. This was the first essential and one that could not be ignored. Therefore a major part of our shipbuilding potential was devoted exclusively to providing sufficient escort vessels for this long drawn-out battle. Escort ships at this time were of several different types, each class being related to the needs and circumstances prevailing when they were laid down. The little corvettes were not much more than glorified whalers with a 4-inch gun and depth charges. From these corvettes were developed slightly larger and more efficient types: the 'River' class frigates (with subsequent US and Canadian built equivalents: the 'Colony' and 'Captain' classes of destroyer-escorts); all these and the later 'Loch' class frigates were essentially anti-submarine vessels of low speed and very slight anti-aircraft potential. The Pacific area of operations had already shown itself to be principally a theatre for aerial warfare. The Japanese submarine fleet, although large, had never proved a formidable opponent. This was mainly due to the way in which it was used: the Japanese disdained to use their underseas fleet to attack merchant shipping unless it was of the

49

type used for carrying troops; instead they used their submarines almost exclusively to attack the heavily escorted capital ships. In this policy, which they pursued right through the war, they achieved some isolated successes but suffered heavy losses in the process.[1] By 1944 the main need for escort vessels allocated to the Pacific was for heavy AA armament rather than AS capability, in which the Western Approaches escorts excelled; for this reason most of the above types were unsuited for the Pacific.

With a view to possible Pacific service in the future, about half the 'Loch' class were converted while building to carry heavier gun armaments and were renamed the 'Bay' class, but they were completed too late to be of use. Only one class of Atlantic escort possessed the heavy AA capability required for Pacific service, the 'Black Swan' class of sloops. They lacked high speed, but were otherwise quite suitable, especially for fleet train work. In the main, however—although a few of this type did reach the Pacific and two full flotillas were allocated to that area—the bulk of them were employed on purely anti-submarine duties in the North Atlantic. They rendered great service in this theatre, in particular while serving with Captain Walker's escort group, but it was still a pity to allocate these ships to the North Atlantic when more suitable anti-submarine vessels were then available.

The second major task to which the Royal Navy was committed was the actual reconquest of Western Europe. This could only be carried out by major amphibious assaults to put the fighting armies ashore, as it was quickly made clear that massed 'Thousand Bomber Raids' had as little effect on the German civilians' will to continue the war as had the Blitz on Britain's population, despite many predictions to the contrary by the Air Chiefs. Apparently Germany could also 'take it'. To provide the large quantities of landing craft and specialised amphibious vehicles required for such major landings, yet another slice of our shipbuilding potential was committed. And we were not only tied up with regard to new construction; numerous fast merchant ships, eminently suitable for fleet auxiliary work, were taken in hand for conversion to landing ships, headquarters ships and the like, again reducing the number available for the Pacific. Also tied up with these projected

[1] An interesting point this: the oft quoted 'chivalry' of the German armed forces allowed the unrestricted U-boat campaign against Merchant ships, while the 'barbarous' Japanese refrained from such a policy. In total war the German method was certainly the most effective and is now accepted, but it does reflect a basic difference in the attitudes of both nations.

An Avenger en route for Pangkalan Brandan　　　　　　　[*Commander Hay*

Task Force 57. *Indomitable* is in the foreground with *Formidable* beyond her   [*Imperial War Museum*

The deck park after a strike   [*Commander Hay*

landings was the fact that the Navy had to supply the bulk of the heavy bombarding ships, mainly old battleships and cruisers, and also the necessary covering squadrons and so on, all of which had to be provided from the Home or Mediterranean Fleets. And, of course, similar requirements had had to be met during the North African landings in November 1942 and in the subsequent invasion of Sicily the following year, for the Italians at that stage still had a powerful fleet in being; although they had shown no aggressive spirit up to that time, there was always the chance that they would sortie out in defence of their homeland.

Thirdly there was the increasingly complicated burden of providing protection for the ever-growing numbers of convoys carrying war material to North Russia. Here the Royal Navy was forced to tie up all its modern warships in order to oppose any attack by the German navy's capital ships based in Norway. Although the actual numbers of ships the Germans had ready for combat varied from time to time, we could not ignore them, as they could always include the heavy ships *Tirpitz, Scharnhorst, Lutzow* and *Admiral Scheer*, supported by the cruisers *Hipper, Nurnberg* and *Koln*, with a dozen big destroyers to call on. Our Home Fleet could not be reduced at all until and unless some of these big capital ships had been eliminated.

It must be remembered that the only modern battleships we had able to stand up to the German giants or, more to the point, of catching them, were the four remaining 'King George V's'. Work had been started on a reduced 'Lion' type battleship—redesigned to carry some of the spare 15-inch mountings then available and named *Vanguard*—but it was at a low priority and work proceeded at a very slow rate.

The RAF, despite many claims to the contrary, had proved itself almost completely incapable of hitting warships at sea with heavy bombers, as indeed had all the other nation's air forces, and had only slowly developed a torpedo-bomber force. Even when it came to hitting stationary targets like battleships moored in harbour, a target long declared ideal bomber bait by the supporters of the heavy bomber, the RAF had shown that for a considerable expenditure of high explosive little results were forthcoming. While the *Scharnhorst* and *Gneisenau* were bottled up in Brest during the winter of 1941–42 massive and prolonged raids were mounted against them by Bomber Command which practically razed the surrounding area, with its civilian population, but only slight damage was done to the two ships and aircraft losses were heavy. The debacle which followed when the two ships made their famous channel dash the following spring was typical. Of the 242 bombers despatched by the RAF, 188 returned *without sighting the enemy at all* and this was in the English Channel.[1] Of the remainder, 39 attacked German and British ships indiscriminately, but caused little damage to either.

It can be readily understood then that there was little which could be done throughout 1942 and 1943 to form an effective force to face the Japanese. Gradually, however, maritime policy took fruit in home waters. With the Salerno landings and the surrender of the Italian fleet, the Mediterranean was made secure. The German navy was equally reduced to impotence during this period: the *Scharnhorst* was caught and sunk off the North Cape by the Home Fleet and the *Tirpitz* was heavily damaged and relegated to a role as shore battery after an attack by midget submarines. The momentous decision taken by Hitler—after a small British force had thrashed his powerful battle-squadron in the Battle of the Barents Sea—that all his remaining heavy ships should be withdrawn to the Baltic was of course unknown here, but a slackening of surface efforts against the Russian convoys was evident. Again, although the enemy's submarines were never completely eliminated from the world's oceans, in mid-1943 there was fought a number of actions along the convoy routes from which the Allied escort forces emerged victorious, having inflicted severe losses on the German U-boat arm.

By late 1943, then, it had become practical to consider the assembly of a new force for the Pacific but a formidable number of obstacles still confronted the planners at the Admiralty.

As related previously, modern warships need to be designed for specific areas of operation if they are to be really effective. Up till now the Navy had concentrated on the North Atlantic and Arctic areas; it followed, therefore, that our modern warships would need a number of both major and minor alterations to enable them to work in tropical seas.

Even at this stage of the war there was still an acute shortage of light anti-aircraft weapons, in particular of the 40-mm Bofors gun. This weapon had proved itself the best of the great variety

[1] Which surely demonstrates the absurdity of the recent Government plan to defend the entire Indian Ocean with fifty F-III's; and the plan's subsequent cancellation for reasons of cost does nothing to diminish this conviction.

of close-range weapons adopted by the Royal Navy but our ships had to rely a great deal on the 20-mm Oerlikon gun which was known to be too small to break up aircraft.

Again, the reliance of the Fleet Air Arm on converted RAF types for their modern aircraft meant that most of the squadrons eventually embarked on Pacific fleet carriers had to be re-equipped with US Navy types, as the Seafires and their like had neither the range nor the ruggedness required for protracted naval warfare.

The conversion of the ships themselves took time, although at least some of the work was rushed through without care; for example, it was found in some destroyers, after they had been operating in eastern waters, that the fans fitted to reduce humidity below decks had been fixed so that they ran backwards reducing their usefulness to practically nil. Even so, it was not these necessary alterations which caused the main delays in the formation of a Pacific fleet.

It might be thought that the loss to the British of territories of such value as Borneo, Malaya, Burma and Hong Kong would have been sufficient justification for the return of the British fleet to the Far East, but many people here, and in the United States also, cast grave doubts firstly on the necessity of our fighting back at all, and secondly on our ability to do so. It was often pointed out, and especially in American circles, that the US Navy was by this time showing itself to be quite capable of thrashing the Japanese on their own. This was further to be emphasised by the great sea battles of 1944. But Churchill was quite determined, as he made clear, to ensure that once the war was over there would be no cause for the Americans to claim that Great Britain had not pulled her weight in the defeat of Japan. With his great historical perception, he could foresee that conditions in the area after the war were likely to be different to the passive stability of the pre-war era, although it is doubtful if even a Solomon could have foreseen the subsequent wholesale retreat from all our obligations in that sphere which has so recently been concluded.

Many millions of British subjects had witnessed the most inglorious defeats ever suffered by British arms and the rapid expulsion of the hitherto 'invincible' white man from their Asian dominions by Asiatics had naturally made an overwhelming impression on them. It is perhaps debatable whether in fact it would not have been wiser to have used all our resources in reconquering these territories instead of duplicating the United States effort against Japan proper. We were in fact heavily pressed to do just that by the Americans, although their motives in so doing were not founded on support for the British Empire. It must be remembered that although national prestige no longer appears to retain much sway in modern Britain, in Asia in the 1940's it was still vastly important not to lose face. The ultimate surrender of the Japanese occupation forces in the former British colonial empire was a very tame affair compared with Japan's fighting victory of three years earlier and made no similar impression. It is perhaps no coincidence that the increasing belligerence of the Asiatic nations towards Europe should have gathered such force during this period, even allowing for the fanning of the hate as part of Communist expansion policies.

Even when we had decided finally that the best help we could send to the Far East was a modern fleet, there was still considerable American opposition to overcome. President Roosevelt appeared enthusiastic enough at the time this plan was first broached, but the American military leaders had grave doubts on the advisability of a British role in the area as a whole. Admiral King has been held up as the prime mover of opposition to British participation on military grounds, but in fairness it must be stated that he was mainly concerned about the effect our collaboration would have on his own resources and facilities—which he assumed would have to be depleted in order to make up British deficiencies. He had built the United States Navy up to an unprecedented strength in three short years and was naturally proud of their vast achievements, power and efficiency. His fears about the inability of the Royal Navy to fully support themselves in Pacific operations without assistance were frequently to be borne out in practice. This shortcoming was to some extent due to the Ministry of War Transport rather than the Admiralty and the Navy, it should be said. In the event this opposition was overcome and when the two fleets did eventually come to work together there was at operational level a general enthusiasm on both sides and mutual benefit was obtained by both sides from experience of each other's methods and equipment.

King, however, always had a rooted antipathy to placing United States naval forces under British command [Admiral Cunningham wrote in his memoirs in connection with the North African landings], though he raised no objection to British forces and units being under United States command when he thought it fit and proper.[1]

Later in his memoirs, Admiral Cunningham returns to King's attitude when the operations of the British Pacific Fleet were under top level discussions:

> Admiral King, adamant as ever, hotly refused to have anything to do with it, and tried to persuade us that the President's acceptance of the offer did not mean what had been said. King, with the other American Chiefs of Staff against him, eventually gave way, but with a very bad grace.[1]

A more detached view is recorded by Admiral Schoefield:

> Admiral King is generally credited with wishing to prevent the British Fleet from operations in the Pacific for purely selfish reasons, and this is certainly the impression he managed to convey to Admiral Cunningham. But in extenuation of his attitude it can be said that he knew better than anyone else the immense superiority of the United States Forces in the area and he was undoubtedly right about the importance of setting up a stable government in Japanese occupied territories as soon as possible after liberation.[2]

Disregarding for the moment Admiral King, the general opinion on co-operation between the Allies was that it could not have been better.

> I must quickly place it on record [Admiral Cunningham says later] that the attitude of the United States Navy in the Pacific was extremely different. Headed by its Commander-in-Chief Admiral Chester W. Nimitz, the American Fleet welcomed us with open arms and gave us all the help in its power. It was not merely polite language when, in January 1945, he directed one of his liaison officers with the British Fleet to tell Admiral Fraser: 'We will make it work regardless of anything.'[1]

Admiral Fraser had been worried about the comparatively junior rank of the chief liaison officer he wished to send to Nimitz's headquarters. He had unhappy recollections of some senior commanders who simply would not deal directly with low-ranking representatives, with resulting delays in communication—General MacArthur was not above reproach in this matter. Fraser was much reassured when Nimitz replied that he did

---

[1] *A Sailor's Odyssey* (Hutchinson, 1950).
[2] *British Sea Power* (Batsford, 1967).

not care what rank the liaison man was. 'If you send me an admiral,' Nimitz told him, 'he'll want a secretary and a flag lieutenant; if you send me a commander, he'll do all the work himself.' And Nimitz was as good as his word. Protocol was never allowed to intervene between the British and American Command. On the British side, much of the credit for the successful Allied co-operation is due to Commander Hopkins and Captain Le Fanu, the head of the liaison team.

It will not be out of place to remark on the helpfulness of the American authorities both at Manus and Ulithi [Vice-Admiral Sir Bernard Rawlings wrote in his report]. I trust we did not ask for their assistance until we were faced with problems which frankly seemed beyond us, but whenever we did so appeal it was responded to with the utmost vigour. I have yet to find a more helpful and re-sponsive attitude than that accorded to me by those American authorities responsible for the provisions and movements of life-guard submarines and aircraft.

Without the generous help of the United States bases [Admiral Vian records], fuelling facilities and spare parts, the Fleet would have been hard set to keep going.

To sum up, Admiral of the Fleet Lord Fraser of North Cape in a recent discussion of the operations of the British Pacific Fleet gave unreserved acknowledgment to the wholehearted and ample scale of help, aid and assistance given to the BPF from everyone in the American Combat Fleets from Admiral Nimitz all the way down. This was an aspect of the operations which, looking back, he particularly wished to emphasise.

Agreement on Britain's contribution was finally reached at the Sextant Conference held in November 1943; it had been hoped at that time that our main fleet would be ready in mid-1944 when it could assist in the planned reconquest of the Philippines. As we shall see, the unforeseen acceleration of the Americans' advance led them far beyond these objectives by the time our forces were ready for operations. In any case the British fleet was not ready on time. The old bug-bear of the fleet train was to prove the stumbling block, and on this all early hopes came to grief.

Obviously the United States would co-operate, but it was Australia which would provide the main bases from which the BPF and its supporting units would work and initial preparations included the despatch and stock-piling of essential stores and equipment there. The Americans had been doing this since 1942 and were by this time well organised, but it had been stipulated that the BPF would need to be self-supporting and we would have to start, even with the powerful assistance of Australia herself, virtually from scratch. The long years of preoccupation with the now abandoned Singapore base were a bitter mockery of our new efforts to build up a fleet in Australia. The heavy drain in ships and men on our Mercantile Marine caused by over four years of unrestricted submarine warfare left very little to spare to allow for the formation of fleet support on the lavish American scale. The British Isles had to have first consideration and then there were our armies in Italy, Burma and, by mid-1944, in France as well. Great Britain was rapidly facing a man-power shortage.

Despite this some progress was made and in September 1944 at the Octagon Conference in Quebec it was stated that our supply force was adequate to ensure the efficiency of our operational fleet. This statement was made in good faith on the assumption that our ships would be engaged off the Philippines, some two thousand miles from Sydney. With the renewal of the American offensive in October and its rapid success, the distance to the war zone was almost doubled: the next objective was now Okinawa. This upset British calculations and we had not the resources to allow for rapid changes to our basic requirements so as to keep up with the fast-moving Americans. In particular, there was a woeful shortage of fast tankers and these were to prove the cornerstone of Pacific operations, where fleets stayed at sea for periods of fifty to sixty days at a time. The standard British techniques for oiling at sea were also obsolete and time-absorbing; this fact also was to provide many a headache. It was soon obvious that, as Admiral King had foreseen, the British fleet would be dependent—to a much larger extent than envisaged in Britain—on a generous interpretation of the scale of co-operation laid down by the planners for Anglo-American aid.

The fact that this aid was given very liberally did not prevent the fuel problem becoming a major source of anxiety for the C-in-C of the BPF in all subsequent sorties.

In February a British naval mission headed by Rear-Admiral C. S. Daniel was sent to the United States and later to the Pacific war zone to study American methods. Work was also started on other preparatory activities; for example the Torres Strait between

Australia's north coast and New Guinea had to be widened and deepened to allow the passage of battleships from the Indian Ocean.

All this work proceeded apace but the establishment of the main base at Sydney took longer than expected. In addition, allowance had to be made for the setting up of intermediate bases between Sydney and the combat area. Several choices were made, but in the end—due to its expediency and the generosity of our ally, the American base at Manus in the Admiralty Islands was made available.[1] No British base could have been made ready before October 1945, such was the backwardness of our organisation. There were no British equivalents to the American Seabee construction units, a special unit of the US Navy which could transform a desolate coral atoll into a first class base in a matter of weeks.

It will be convenient at this point to plot the American operations which led to the conquest of the Philippines, as this was the final factor in determining the Royal Navy's theatre of operations.

After the Battle of the Philippine Sea in June 1944 when the United States Navy had smashed Japan's new air fleets and forced the enemy to retire to his home islands and Malayan bases, the Japanese prepared themselves for one last mighty effort; their entire naval strength, still very great, was to be committed to this. The rapidity with which one American assault followed another had now got the Japanese planners seriously worried and so accordingly plans were also made to defend to the death their final links with the rich oil regions of the south, should the Americans drive that far. These areas had been the prime objective during Japan's initial assaults and should the United States succeed in driving a wedge between these rich islands and Japan herself all would be lost as their war machine would grind to a halt. Without oil, there could be no major offensive.

It was clear to the Japanese that the Philippines would be the key to their defence of oil supplies and for that reason would very likely be the next Allied target; however, they doubted if the Americans would attack here without taking prior steps to occupy some of the neighbouring islands and this they felt would give

[1] It should be noted that the Admiralty Islands were British territory.

them sufficient warning. Indeed, this was the American intention right up to the last moment, but almost at the eleventh hour the Fast Carrier Force caused these plans to be abandoned.

The great strength of the American Task Groups had enabled the United States Navy to smash all land-based opposition during their drive across the Pacific, but this opposition had been limited. They were now determined to test their effectiveness against the most powerful shore-based defences the enemy had in the south-west area. Heavy and prolonged strikes were put in during early October by the Third Fleet against Formosa, Okinawa and the chain of linking airfields between them. The Japanese would have to use these islands as staging posts to fly fresh aircraft down to any threatened area from their home islands, and so they were strongly defended.

The US Navy planes swarmed over all these bases and inflicted severe damage to them as well as creating havoc amongst the enemy's offshore shipping in the China Sea, which had considered itself immune behind its island chain. Between the tenth and fourteenth of October the Third Fleet's aircrews claimed to have destroyed over five hundred enemy aircraft in combat and on their airstrips and to have sunk 50,000 tons of enemy shipping.

The Japanese, after recovering from their initial shock, reacted strongly. They sent in heavy strikes against the Third Fleet, but so effective had the fleet's defences become, that they inflicted only light damage. The cruiser *Canberra* was the only major casualty; she was hit by an aerial torpedo late on the 13th and was taken in tow. Admiral Halsey deliberately chose this course instead of sinking her and withdrawing at speed, in the hope of luring the enemy to commit everything he had in his attempts to destroy Halsey's fleet. The Japanese swallowed the bait and renewed air attacks on an even larger scale against the American ships. Again an enormous toll was taken of the assailants, the Americans only suffering some damage to the cruiser *Houston* and minor hits on one or two other vessels. The Japanese, for their part, so exaggerated their claims that a powerful surface force sortied from Japan to finish off the 'tattered remnants of the United States Task Force'.[1] However, subsequently this force learnt that the Americans were untouched, with twelve carriers and supporting

[1] Quoted from an intercepted Japanese propaganda release, broadcast soon after the engagement.

battleships, and prudently withdrew before the Americans could launch an air strike against them. . . .

Air assaults on a diminishing scale continued throughout the 15th and 16th October, by which time the enemy's newly-arrived reserves had been completely exhausted. The Third Fleet then sent its bombers and fighters against the main Japanese air bases on Luzon in the Philippines to test reaction.

The enormous losses inflicted on Japan in this and the previous strikes had so reduced the potential of the Japanese air fleets that the Americans concluded that their invasion forces would meet no heavy opposition at all. Accordingly rapid changes were made in the grand plan which resulted in the advancement of the Philippines' invasion date to the 20th October. At ten a.m. the first troops waded ashore: General MacArthur had returned.

This was the moment the Japanese had dreaded and again they were caught on the wrong foot. All their available surface units were hastily oiled and prepared to carry out the long awaited master plan for a final reckoning with the Americans. In the meantime, the Japanese troops in the Philippines toughened their resistance and fought with their usual fanatical devotion. As it had become increasingly obvious that conventional air strikes were no longer effective against the strong Task Forces, the Japanese were now forced to fall back on their last resort, suicide attacks. The suicide planes were at first manned only by volunteers, of which there were always an overwhelming number, but it rapidly became an established part of the Japanese defence and there was no lack of young men ready to die for their Emperor by crashing his aircraft into an Allied warship. Among the first victims of the *Kamikazes*—named after the Divine Wind which had wrecked a Mongol invasion fleet in ancient times—was the Australian heavy cruiser *Australia* acting as part of the offshore supporting squadron giving fire cover to the beach-heads. A suicide bomber crashed into her bridge killing her captain and causing much damage so that she was forced to withdraw all the way to Manus to effect repairs. As yet the scale of these attacks had not caused very heavy casualties, but the Kamikazes were soon to become the Allies' major enemy. In the original Japanese plan the suicide raids were designed merely to supplement the grand attack. But the very nature of this manned-missile, so alien to Western minds, provoked a strong reaction and led the Allies to take an extremely serious view of the damage such methods might achieve. Perhaps

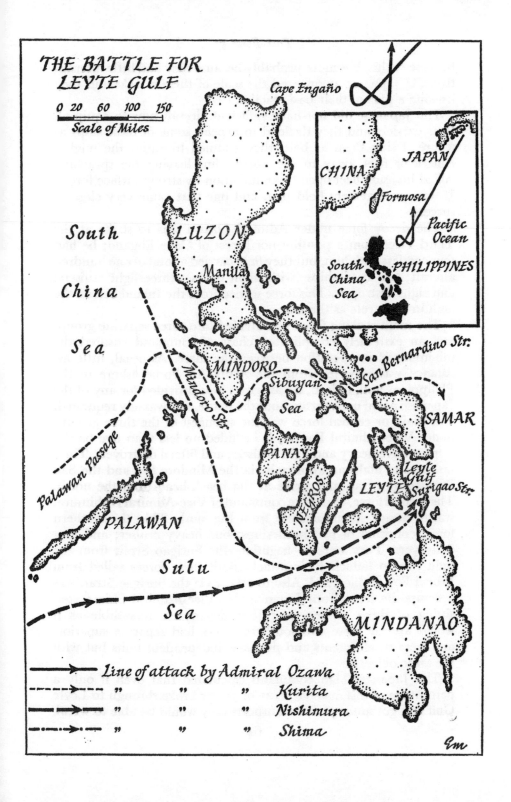

THE BATTLE FOR
LEYTE GULF

0 20   60   100   150
Scale of Miles

Cape Engaño

CHINA

JAPAN

Formosa

Pacific
Ocean

South
China
Sea

PHILIPPINES

South

China

Sea

LUZON

Manila

MINDORO

Mindoro Str.

Sibuyan
Sea

San Bernardino Str.

SAMAR

Palawan Passage

PANAY

NEGROS

Leyte
Gulf
LEYTE   Surigao Str.

PALAWAN

Sulu

Sea

MINDANAO

Line of attack by Admiral Ozawa
    "   "   "   Kurita
    "   "   "   Nishimura
    "   "   "   Shima

Em

because of this, but more probably because they had little alternative, the Japanese augmented the scale of these attacks and they became a part of their basic tactics.

The Japanese did not have sufficient aircraft now to equip all their carriers and they decided to expend some of these ships as a lure. Using them as bait, they planned to entice the mighty American fleet away to the north, thus leaving the sprawling Allied invasion fleet open to annihilation by strong surface forces. It was an extremely bold plan and one that came very close to success.

The decoy force under Admiral Ozawa was to strike at the Third Fleet from a position north-east of Cape Engano; he had four carriers with him, but they only carried a total of one hundred aircraft; two battleships (with flight decks); three light cruisers; and eight destroyers. This force sortied from the Inland Sea on the 20th in their role as the bait.

The main striking force was divided into three separate groups and an extremely complicated chain of command ensured the minimum of co-operation between the three. As usual, little assistance was expected from the Army Air Force ashore in the Philippines and, indeed, no air cover was provided for any of the Japanese naval units throughout the battle, nor was any requested. The main or central force was the strongest of the three groups: under Vice-Admiral Kurita, it included no less than five battleships, twelve heavy and light cruisers, and fifteen destroyers. Their task was to make an approach via the Mindoro Sea and the San Bernardino Strait and strike at the beach-head from the north. The second force, under the command of Vice-Admiral Nishimura, was to attack simultaneously from the south. This, the southern force, consisted of two battleships; one heavy cruiser; and four destroyers. They were to negotiate the Surigao Strait from the Sulu Sea to launch their attack. Both these forces sailed from Brunei Bay on the 22nd. Also to attack via the Surigao Strait was a composite force from Japan under Vice-Admiral Shima consisting of three cruisers and four destroyers. Incredible as it would appear these two southern forces had separate superiors and were to all intents and purposes independent units but with the same objective.

The Japanese high command calculated that even if only a percentage of this massive array of power broke through to Leyte Gulf and got amongst the transports they would be able to wreak complete destruction and chaos upon the invasion fleet and their supporting warships.

Although this American support squadron included six to eight old battleships, several cruisers and dozens of destroyers and escorts and no less than sixteen escort-carriers, most of these ships were equipped as shore gunfire support vessels and stocks of armour-piercing shell were low; the little carriers had few heavy bombs or torpedoes for their bombers. Therefore, in a straight fight with the Japanese forces ranged against them they would be at heavy disadvantage. They relied for their protection from the Japanese Navy on Halsey's Third Fleet which now comprised no less than fifteen carriers, eight modern battleships, thirteen cruisers and fifty-eight destroyers. This massive concentration was operating to the east of the Philippines in four task groups. By bad luck one of these groups was despatched to Ulithi on the 22nd to replenish and was five hundred miles away before it could be recalled.

Vice-Admiral Kurita's force soon ran into trouble when it stumbled into an American submarine patrol line in the south Palawan Passage on the 23rd. Here they lost the cruisers *Maya* and *Atago* sunk and the *Takao* damaged for the loss of just one US boat, the *Darter*.

Admiral Shima's force was also detected early on, but Ozawa's decoy force had penetrated to within striking range of the most northerly US Task Force undetected by the 24th.

The tracking of the Japanese battleship force into the Sulu Sea at once initiated the recall of the fourth Task Force and preparations were made in the other three to strike at this enemy. Before these strikes could be assembled the US ships were subjected to strong and persistent attacks from Japanese planes from the Philippines. Thus the Third Fleet was heavily engaged throughout the morning of the 24th. They escaped severe damage, except for the loss of the carrier *Princeton* and damage to several cruisers and destroyers which went to her aid. Added to these shore-based attacks came the strikes from the still undetected Japanese carriers to the north.

Admiral Halsey quite naturally regarded the presence of enemy carriers as his greatest danger and searches were flown off, but it was not until dusk that Ozawa's force was sighted, too late for an attack to be mounted against them. The rest of the 24th was therefore spent in directing heavy strikes against the enemy battleships steaming through the Sibuyan Sea.

Despite intense bombing by the US planes the only enemy casualty was the giant battleship *Musashi* which sank after taking twenty or so torpedoes and about forty bombs; the heavy cruiser *Myoko* was damaged and returned to Singapore. In the afternoon Kurita reversed course and the American airmen reported that they had inflicted heavy losses on the enemy and that he was retiring.

Admiral Halsey therefore considered that the main battleship force was no longer a threat to the transports and towards dusk set off with his entire strength in pursuit of the enemy carriers far to the north.

This was exactly in accordance with the Japanese plan. At 5 p.m. Kurita, his strength hardly reduced, reversed course once again and made for Leyte Gulf.

The southern Japanese force had been tracked throughout the day and preparations to meet it had been made by Admiral Oldendorf's squadron, formed from the bombarding warships; under his command he had six old battleships, eight cruisers and twenty-eight destroyers. These lay in wait across the northern mouth of the Surigao Strait. And into the muzzles of this concentration of fire steamed *both* the isolated Japanese squadrons. Only one destroyer survived from Nishimura's force, while Shima's ships were badly cut up. This effectively finished off any enemy assault via the Mindanao Sea.

The landing forces at Leyte Gulf must, by the morning of the 25th, have been supremely confident that they were immune from any assault. By mis-chance, an error of signalling had led Admiral Kinkaid at Leyte to believe that Admiral Halsey had left a strong battleship force guarding the entrance of the San Bernardino Strait, in case the enemy repeated his attempts to force this passage. In fact, all the powerful battleships of the Third Fleet were far away to the north, where they had indeed been formed into a striking force, but with the object of catching and destroying Ozawa's decoy force of fleeing carriers.

Kurita's squadron emerged from the San Bernardino Strait on that same morning and steamed into the open waters off Samar expecting a fight; instead he found himself unopposed. Much relieved, he set course for the landing beaches.

At 6.45 a.m. on the 25th October, with the effect of a bombshell, Admiral Kurita's force was first sighted; it consisted then of four battleships, eight cruisers and eleven destroyers.

Operating off the beach-head, the Americans had three groups of escort carriers providing air support for the troops ashore; it was the planes of the most northerly of these groups which sighted Kurita's ships. Within a short time the group was under heavy gunfire from the enemy battleships. Incredulous disbelief was soon changed to frantic action as the Japanese salvos started to arrive, and all available aircraft were flown off armed with whatever was available in a desperate attempt to harry the enemy and throw his aim out. At the same time urgent signals reflecting the panic in the air were flying to and fro across the vast arena of the battle.

Admiral Oldendorf's battleships were the only ships near enough to ward off this threat, but they were still rearming and resting after their night engagement and had to replenish their armour-piercing shell. They were got under way as quickly as possible, but even so they would have been little match for the Japanese squadron in daylight. It is in fact doubtful whether they would have reached the beach-head in time. All aircraft from the other two escort carrier groups were put into the air and made repeated strafing attacks and bombing runs on the enemy. Meanwhile, calls were sent out in plain language to Admiral Halsey asking the whereabouts of the battleships of the fast carrier forces.

Despite all these efforts there seems little doubt that Kurita could have scored an overwhelming victory, but he was irresolute at this critical moment and did not press home his attack. In fairness to him there was much to conceal from him that success was in his grasp. He knew of the annihilation of the southern force; he was unaware that Ozawa had been so successful in luring away Halsey's ships. He initially mistook the little 17-knot escort carriers for fleet carriers and approached them very cautiously; this allowed them to get home some heavy air strikes which caused the loss of three of his cruisers before his gunfire started to take effect.

At 7.30 a.m. the seven destroyers screening the northerly carrier group attacked him most courageously in order to divert his attention. Approaching to within point-blank range they were heavily hit and three were sunk, but they managed to damage another cruiser and so to add to Kurita's problems.

Nevertheless, by 9 a.m. his force had virtually trapped the carrier group and his heavy gunfire was beginning to take deadly effect. One of the carriers was sunk. The others owe their survival to their flimsy hulls, as the big armour-piercing shells frequently passed straight through them without exploding. Even so, it appeared that they must be doomed, but then, at 9.25, the Japanese force was seen to retire northwards. After three further hours of aimless counter-marching under constant air attack Kurita finally decided to withdraw. For the Americans it was truly a miracle; for the Japanese it was the throwing away of their last chance of achieving a major victory.

Meantime, away to the north-east, Halsey had been getting in heavy air strikes at the decoy force and, besides sinking one carrier, had damaged three others; the Third Fleet's battleships were within forty miles of the enemy. History seemed about to be given an ironic twist: the battleships of the original American fleet had been destroyed at the start of the war by Japanese carriers; now the remaining enemy carriers faced annihilation by the new US battleships. But it was not to be. At 11.15 the racing battleships were called off from the 30-knot hunt and course was reversed in answer to the frantic appeals from Leyte Gulf, although it was by then far too late for them to render assistance. And so it was left once more to the fleet carriers to finish off the fleeing enemy; throughout the day they sent in several strikes against them, and succeeded in sinking all the remaining enemy carriers, although the two battleships of Ozawa's force escaped unscathed.

The scattered ships of the mighty Japanese fleet were now pursued by the Americans throughout the 26th and a few cripples were finished off. Thus ended the most decisive naval battle in modern history and certainly by far the largest. It proved to be the end of the Japanese navy as a major force. But the Japanese plan had come within an ace of working and several major holes had been revealed in the American command structure.

The Japanese now had to fall back on their one remaining trick—the Kamikazes. As we have noted these were meant to co-operate by co-ordinating their efforts with the surface attack, but in effect they failed to do so. On the 25th, however, they made their mark after Kurita's retirement; their attacks caused the sinking of one more escort carrier and severe damage to six others. Throughout the rest of the Philippines campaign the number of sorties mounted and so did the damage they managed to inflict: no less than seven fleet carriers were hit at one time or another off the Philippines and one, the *Intrepid*, was hit five times. None of these ships were sunk but, with their wooden flight decks, heavy damage was inevitable and they were forced to withdraw from the

Pangkalan Brandan under attack

Marshalling aircraft – Corsairs on *Victorious*   [*Commander Hay*

Preparing for take off   [*Commander Hay*

front line for months to effect repairs while loss of life was heavy. Fortunately for the US Navy their huge warship construction programme enabled them to make good their losses and the Third Fleet remained a powerful force throughout the rest of the campaign.

Counter measures were taken against the Kamikazes which included the carrying of larger numbers of fighter aircraft to maintain stronger combat air patrols overhead, while special radar-fitted destroyers were stationed as distant-warning pickets to give advanced information of incoming raids.

As a result of this great victory the doubts about the need for the planned British contribution were once again brought up. With the Japanese surface fleet in eclipse it was argued that the British contribution was now superfluous. As by this date the British fleet had actually been assembled in the Indian Ocean many expressed the opinion that it would be better employed in acting, as the US Third Fleet had done in the Pacific, as the sledge-hammer to open the way for the re-conquest of the former British territories rather than in the final drive on Japan.

These ideas, of course, found little favour in British Naval circles, it was felt here that now that an efficient force had at last been assembled, in the opinion of many for the first time in the war, then it would clearly be a futile waste of a first class weapon to use it in a secondary theatre of operations. They wished it to be used where it deserved to be, in the front line of battle; not relegated to a back area as a mopping-up force. They were particularly anxious to show that the Royal Navy, once properly equipped, was a match for the Japanese in straight conflict and was the equal of the United States Navy in performance if no longer in size. In all this they had the backing of the Prime Minister and in the end this view prevailed.

4

Renewal of the Offensive

The nucleus of the British Pacific Fleet was formed from the more modern ships of the East Indies Fleet based in the Indian Ocean under the command of Admiral Somerville. Since the beginning of 1944 this fleet had been steadily reinforced in preparation for the long planned assaults on Rangoon and other parts of South East Asia, but lack of sufficient landing-craft had led to repeated postponements of these objectives. Despite these setbacks, the East Indies Fleet had started, in a limited way, to carry out offensive operations against the Japanese in this vast arena—operations which were to provide useful background knowledge for future Pacific operations. Modelling itself on the Fast Carrier Task Forces of the United States Fleet, but in miniature and mainly with older ships, they took part in several pin-prick raids on the enemy's flank, which although they failed to divert the enemy's attention westward in any strength, tied down a percentage of his reserves and laid a foundation for future operations.

Early in 1944 the battleships *Queen Elizabeth* and *Valiant*, the fleet carrier *Illustrious*, together with some modern cruisers and destroyers, arrived on station under the command of Admiral Sir Arthur J. Power, second-in-command of the BPF, who was flying his flag in the battle-cruiser *Renown*. All three capital ships were old, but they had been modernised to some extent; unfortunately, the carrier was still equipped with the Barracuda bomber, which reduced her effective strike capacity. The carriers *Formidable*, *Indomitable* and *Victorious* were also promised as reinforcements, but were not yet available. To compensate in some way for this the light carrier *Unicorn*[1] and two escort carriers, *Shah* and *Begum*, were

---

[1] *Unicorn* was actually built as a repair ship for Fleet Air Arm aircraft and to carry spares, but she had the dimensions and armament of a light fleet carrier and was frequently used in this capacity in her early operations with the fleet, notably at Salerno and in the Indian Ocean.

added to the strength. Further, as a temporary measure while the main Japanese naval strength lay at Singapore, the Americans agreed to the loan of the carrier *Saratoga* and three destroyers to further bolster our fleet in case the enemy repeated his earlier sortie westwards.

In actual fact the Japanese had far too much on their hands in the Pacific, but Somerville had no intention of allowing this un-expected surfeit of strength to be wasted. He planned to put into effect a long cherished operation, a carrier attack against the Japanese naval base at Sabang on the north-east tip of Sumatra. With the arrival of further reinforcements in the shape of the French battleship *Richelieu* and the Dutch cruiser *Tromp*, this operation was put into effect in April, designed to coincide with General MacArthur's assault on Hollandia.

Somerville sailed from Trincomalee on the 16th of that month with four battleships, two carriers, six cruisers and fourteen destroyers; although the bulk of the ships were British, the force included representatives from our three allies and the Common-wealth.

At 5.30 a.m. on the 19th the first air strikes were launched from a position one hundred miles south-west of Sabang. In all forty-six bombers and forty fighters were flown off. They achieved complete surprise when they started their run in on the target at 7 a.m. Oil tanks were destroyed, harbour and airfields were hit, two small merchant ships were destroyed and twenty-four enemy aircraft were written off. The only Allied casualty was an Ameri-can fighter, but the pilot was rescued by a British submarine lying offshore.

The Japanese were caught flat-footed and their reaction was sluggish and ineffective: three enemy torpedo bombers approached the fleet as it withdrew and these were all shot down well clear of the ships.

The success of the sortie led to a repetition the following month. This time the oil refinery at Soerabaya was chosen for the attack and the fleet sailed from Ceylon, in similar strength to the previous operation, on the 6th May. The flying-off position, 180 miles south of the target, was beyond the limited range of the Barracuda so *Illustrious* embarked Avengers for the job. They were soon to prove invaluable and, before long, all the British carriers in the East were to re-equip with them. This time refuelling was carried out in Exmouth Bay, Northern Australia on the 15th. On the 17th

CHINA

Delhi
Karachi
Bombay   INDIA   Calcutta   Mandalay
                                                Akyab   Hainan
                                                BURMA
                                                Rangoon   SIAM   INDO
                          Madras   Bangkok   CHINA
                                      20TH JUNE '44   Andaman Is.   Saigon
                                      17/19TH OCT.'44 Port Blair   Camranh
                  Trincomalee   Nicobar Is.   Bay
        Colombo   Sabang 1
Maldive Is.   CEYLON   19TH APRIL AND   2 3 MALAYA
                              25TH JULY '44   Singapore
Addu Atoll   2ND.JAN '45   Pladjoe BORNEO
                              20TH.NOV'44   Palembang
        Chagos   Songei Gerong
        Archipelago   24TH.JAN '45   Soerabaya
                                      29TH.JAN '45   Batavia   JAVA
    Diego Garcia   17TH.MAY'44

                                        Cocos Is.

                                                        Exmouth Gulf
•Rodriguez Is.   I N D I A N

                     O C E A N

        N   AUSTRALIA

1 Penang 2 Pangkalan Brandan 3 Belawan Deli
◄━━━ British Naval Attacks
▨ Japanese-Occupied Territory
▦ Allied and other Territory
╌╌╌ Approximate Limit of
      Japanese Gains
                                                        Em

May forty-five bombers and forty fighters reached their destination undetected and again opposition was light. Once more all targets were neutralised for the loss of only one plane. A repeat attack was not made at once only because of confusion in communications between the flagship and the carriers; this slip-up made it clear that the Royal Navy still had a great deal to master before they became as efficient as the Americans in large-scale carrier operations, but the attack had again demonstrated the East Indies Fleet's ability to penetrate the Japanese defences in the area with impunity.

The *Saratoga* and her destroyers were withdrawn to the Pacific at the conclusion of this operation but Admiral Somerville was determined to keep up the pressure as far as he possibly could. He still had one carrier and on 20th June the fleet struck again. This time the *Illustrious* used her Barracudas to hit installations at Port Blair in the Andaman islands. Although the damage they inflicted was small materially, due in the main to lack of targets suitable for aerial attack, the enemy was kept guessing as to where and when the next blow would land. Later in the month welcome reinforcements arrived at Ceylon in the shapes of the *Victorious* and *Indomitable* with additional light forces.

Sir James Somerville now had three carriers, but of course the newly arrived ships were raw to tropical operations; to give them combat experience before they sailed to the Pacific it was decided to attack Sabang again, but this time in greater force. It was planned that in addition to air attacks the battleships and cruisers were to play their part by bombarding the harbour and dockside area.

On the 22nd July Somerville put to sea with his strongest fleet to date.

The fleet was made up of the *Illustrious* and *Victorious*; the *Renown*, *Queen Elizabeth* and *Valiant*; the heavy cruiser *Cumberland*; the light cruisers *Tromp*, *Kenya*, *Nigeria*, *Phoebe*, *Ceylon* and *Gambia*; and the destroyers *Quality*, *Quickmatch*, *Quilliam*, *Racehorse*, *Raider*, *Rapid*, *Relentless*, *Rocket*, *Roebuck*, and *Rotherham*. All these ships, except the capital ships and the 8-inch cruiser were modern vessels, a welcome change for Somerville after the dubious selection of warships he had been forced to use previously.

Air strikes from the two carriers went in at dawn on the 25th July to neutralise enemy airfields; in all, eighty Corsairs and nine Barracudas—these latter all came from *Illustrious* and were on their last sortie—were put into the air. Eight of the fighters were to act as spotters for the fleet's gunfire, while a further twelve were to provide a combat air patrol—or CAP—above the fleet. Half the remainder were to hit Koetaradja airfield in Sumatra, while the others were to co-ordinate their strikes on Sabang itself with the fleet bombardment.

Initially poor visibility restricted the fighter sweeps, but they managed to make several runs on their targets, effectively keeping the Japanese aircraft grounded; otherwise they found few worthwhile targets for themselves. The battleships opened fire on the harbour with their 15-inch guns and the huge projectiles began to fall in ear-splitting salvos that shook the whole town. Heavy damage was done to installations and two freighters were sunk. Led by the Dutch cruiser *Tromp* the three 'Quilliam' class destroyers made a sweep into the harbour entrance, firing their torpedoes as they did so and loosing off their 4.7-inch guns over open sights at shore targets. The cruisers closed inshore and shelled shore defences and radar installations. Admiral Somerville described the whole effect as 'spectacular'.

Once more the enemy reaction proved slow and insipid; no British ship suffered any damaged and only one plane was lost, the pilot being rescued by the *Nigeria*. Only a few enemy aircraft attacked the fleet and these were easily destroyed or driven off. The fleet returned to Ceylon in high fettle.

This operation had firmly underlined the new air of determination and confidence which now replaced the marked sense of inferiority that had pervaded the fleet in the dark days of 1942. Sadly this high-spot marked the last assault to be carried out under the command of Admiral Somerville, who had had to bear the brunt of the humiliations of the earlier years. On the return of the fleet to harbour he hauled down his flag to take up his new appointment in America.

He was replaced as C-in-C by the leader designate of the Pacific Fleet, Admiral Sir Bruce Fraser. Admiral Fraser came straight from command of the Home Fleet where his brillant leadership had brought about the destruction of the *Scharnhorst* the previous December. He had the reputation of a fighting admiral and was just the man to command Britain's most powerful naval force. Until sufficient ships of his fleet arrived, he took over command of the East Indies Fleet, to which they were temporarily attached.

It was still thought essential to keep up the tempo of our air strikes in order to toughen up the many still untried aircrews with the carrier squadron which was rapidly increasing in numbers as the supply of American aircraft increased. Therefore during August attacks were made by the carriers *Victorious* and the recently arrived *Formidable* against various targets in Sumatra and, if the results were not spectacular, then the testing of the new equipment was invaluable.

The second-in-command, Admiral Power, took a section of the fleet to sea again on the 15th October for strikes against the Nicobar Islands, an enemy-held group mid-way between the Andaman Islands and Sumatra. Main objective of these attacks was to cause a diversion in the hope of preventing reinforcements being transferred from the Indian Ocean theatre to the Philippines where the previously mentioned American assaults were about to commence. The enemy had already committed all his main resources to halt this offensive and our small blows made no difference to their dispositions, but this, of course, was not known at the time. Only a full-scale offensive and amphibious operations against Malaya or Burma could have caused the Japanese to change their plans, but the Allies were still without sufficient troops, material and landing-craft in South-East Asia to make this feasible.

Air attacks backed up by bombardments were carried out during the three-day period between the 17th and 19th October. Again worthwhile targets were hard to find and this was to cause some frustration among the young airmen eager to make their mark; the ships' gunners, too, were stuck in their sweltering turrets without action for days on end. But the negligible opposition signalled our complete mastery over this area, should we be able to take advantage of it. Unfortunately, an air strike on the Japanese ships at Singapore was not thought practicable; this would have been more to the taste of the fleet.

November saw the official assumption of command of the British Pacific Fleet by Admiral Fraser while Admiral Power took over as commander of the East Indies Fleet. It also saw the arrival of Admiral Sir Philip Vian to assume command of the 1st Aircraft-Carrier Squadron which was to be its backbone.

Like Fraser, Admiral Vian was a fighter, with a reputation in the fleet second to none. The outbreak of war had found him in command as Captain (D) to a flotilla of old World War I destroyers operating into the Atlantic, but he had soon moved on to command of a Home Fleet flotilla, the 4th Destroyer Flotilla which he led from the *Afridi* until she was bombed and sunk beneath him. His exploits aboard her and in the *Cossack* off Norway had earned him undying fame, which his attack with the flotilla on the *Bismarck* the following year only enhanced. Aboard the cruiser *Naiad*, in command of the famous 15th Cruiser Squadron during the black days of 1942, his action off Sirte, during which his little force outfought and outmanoeuvred an Italian battleship and cruiser squadron had earned him wide praise and he was no newcomer to carrier operations. At the invasion of Italy he had been in command of 'Force V', a task group consisting of the carrier *Unicorn*, four escort carriers and three anti-aircraft cruisers. His last post had been that of deputy naval commander afloat aboard the cruiser *Scylla* off Normandy.

The team now forming was going to be a strong one. Vice-Admiral Charles S. Daniel had returned to become Vice-Admiral Administration for the Pacific Fleet. This job was said to be just about the most daunting to be taken on by any naval officer, the complexity of the conflicting demands and availability proved to be enormous. Like Vice-Admiral Vian, Daniel had started the war as Captain (D) of a Home Fleet destroyer flotilla, the 8th, which he led from the destroyer *Faulknor*. From here he had become Director of Plans at the Admiralty during 1940–41, and had thus experienced naval war organisation at first hand. In the *Renown*, he had commanded the task force which escorted the US carrier *Wasp* during her attempts to reinforce Malta by flying off Spitfires to that beleagured island in 1942; this striking piece of Anglo-American cooperation had led to further exacting tasks in the United States and now in Australia. He was to prove himself equal to the job.

A further problem arose when it was realised that the BPF was to operate under overall American command when it reached its war theatre: Admiral Fraser was too senior an officer to be subordinated in this way. It was therefore decided that his second-in-command, Vice-Admiral Sir Bernard Rawlings, would take his place at sea and that Admiral Fraser would perforce have to command his fleet from Australia, or from any subsequent advance base. This he readily agreed to, although it must have been a galling decision.

Vice-Admiral Rawlings had served with distinction as Rear-Admiral Commanding the 1st Battle Squadron in the Mediterranean Fleet under Admiral Cunningham. Here the two men had defeated the superior Italian fleet in every encounter throughout 1940–41 and had held on throughout the grim days of 1942 despite heavy losses inflicted by the German dive-bombers and submarines. Off Crete, in command of the 7th Cruiser Squadron, he had been wounded when his ships were heavily bombed during the evacuation of the troops ashore, and later he had served with the famous 'Force K' at Malta. In addition to these solid achievements, he had experience of the Japanese from his pre-war service.

It was planned eventually to have two cruiser squadrons, the 3rd and 4th, on station and command of these was assumed by Rear-Admiral E. J. Brind and Rear-Admiral R. M. Servaes; command of the destroyer forces, which eventually comprised the 4th, 7th, 24th, 25th, and 27th Flotillas, went to Rear-Admiral J. H. Edelsten. Other major appointments were Rear-Admiral D. B. Fisher as commander of the Fleet Train, which included escort carriers and frigates as well as the diverse assortment of auxiliaries; Rear-Admiral R. H. Portal was to be responsible for the numerous squadrons of Fleet Air Arm aircraft and their shore facilities in Australia.

Meanwhile in the Indian Ocean the monthly British attacks continued, as more and more ships arrived at Ceylon. In November Vice-Admiral Vian sailed to attack the oil refinery at Pangkalan Brandan in Sumatra with the carriers *Indomitable* and *Illustrious*—her bomber squadrons now finally equipped with Avengers; the cruisers *Newcastle*, *Argonaut* and *Black Prince*; and destroyers *Kempenfelt*, *Whirlwind*, *Wrangler*, *Wessex* and *Wakeful*. These ships left Trincomalee on the 17th and, after refuelling at sea on the 18th,[1] had by early on the 20th arrived without being spotted off the mouth of the Malacca Strait to commence 'Operation Outflank'.

The day dawned misty and overcast and prospects for accurate bombing were considered poor. Despite this the air strike of twenty-seven Avengers, escorted by twenty-eight Corsairs and Hellcats was flown off by 7.15 a.m. The weather failed to clear, however, and after attempts at penetrating the murk the main strike was put in at the oil port of Belawan Deli further south where they hit oil storage tanks and harbour installations. They encountered no aerial opposition, the flak was moderate and none of our aircraft were lost.

[1] The fuelling force was the tanker *Wave King* escorted by *Wager* and *Whelp*.

As the fleet reversed course back into the Indian Ocean during the afternoon a further strike was sent against the Japanese airfields at Sabang to let them know they had not been overlooked. Again no British planes were lost and the Task Force then returned to base. This raid proved to be the final assault of 1944 and plans were now well advanced for the fleet's move to the main zone of operations.

On the 4th December, Admiral Fraser flew from Ceylon to Australia, from where he flew on to Pearl Harbour to confer with Admiral Nimitz. In Australia he had found the authorities eager to assist in setting up our facilities, even though the Australians were already considerably extended in supplying the Americans. They were pleased to welcome a strong British fleet again, but it became clear that the scale of support would necessitate our relying on much smaller margins than our ally enjoyed and that our operations would be somewhat handicapped as a result of this.

Nevertheless, everyone seemed willing to make it work. At Pearl Harbour Admiral Fraser reached the final conclusions with Nimitz on the readiness of our fleet and was able to report home that both Admirals Nimitz and Spruance welcomed the BPF as powerful reinforcements. There still remained the question of how and where they would best be employed. The Americans were building up their immense strength for their next big move across the Pacific; they were now approaching Japanese territory and resistance was likely to prove even more fanatical than that previously encountered. Admiral Nimitz wished to use the BPF in conjunction with the Third Fleet to smash this resistance, but there were still many in top American defence circles who considered that the Royal Navy would be unable to keep up with their task forces. They once more put forward the argument that the British fleet should instead operate off the Philippines and assist General MacArthur in his campaigns in that area which were likely to be bloody and protracted.

This was virtually the same argument put forward previously and indeed the re-conquest of the former British territory of Borneo which would automatically follow did seem attractive. The British strongly resisted these pressures, but the Americans could not finally make up their minds. This of course meant additional problems for the administration of the fleet. The United States had readily volunteered base facilities at Manus in the Admiralty

Islands, and this offer was gratefully taken up. It was still a long way from Okinawa and plans were pressed ahead to establish a more convenient staging base in the Philippines. Admiral Fisher started despatching his transports there during December and January.

Following his talks at Pearl Harbour, Admiral Fraser visited the United States Seventh Fleet operating off the Philippines to gain first hand knowledge of the type of resistance his men were likely to encounter in the months ahead. General MacArthur was anxious to enlist Fraser's approval for the operation of the British fleet in support of MacArthur's own land campaigns and he put himself out to charm the British admiral. This idea—to give the BPF a separate role from that of the main US fleet—found favour with a number of the planners at this stage, but Fraser himself was not won over. This partly stemmed from the fact that he very much liked the prospect of working under Nimitz. It was during this visit that he was granted a grandstand view, and narrowly escaped death, when a Kamikaze dived into the bridge structure of the battleship *New Mexico* from where he was watching a bombardment of enemy positions ashore. The Captain of the ship was killed, as was General Lumsden, the British Liaison Officer on MacArthur's staff, and about a hundred others. It was not a good omen for the future and at this time a decidedly gloomy view was taken of the Kamikaze as a major weapon.

It was hoped that our carriers would withstand such attacks better than our allies' ships were able to, but it was also plain that the anti-aircraft batteries of all our ships were far below the requirements of Pacific warfare. During 1944 the further supplies of the 40-mm Bofors gun were being stepped up but in the meantime the ships would have to take on the enemy with what they had.

The bulk of the fleet was now assembled at Ceylon where the ships were undergoing training and refits, but before they finally sailed east Rear-Admiral Vian was given the opportunity to repeat his attack on Pangkalan Brandan as the previous strikes had not inflicted sufficient damage.

Accordingly he sailed on the last day of the year with the carriers *Indomitable*, *Victorious* and the newly arrived *Indefatigable*, the cruisers *Argonaut*, *Black Prince*, *Ceylon*, and *Suffolk* and eight destroyers to execute 'Operation Lentil'. The Japanese failed to sight them during their approach and the aircraft were flown off at first light. This time the weather proved kinder and our squadrons met with clear sky which allowed accurate bombing on the 2nd January. The initial strike of fighters strafed nearby airfields in the now established pattern of attack and then the main force of Avengers with Corsair and Hellcat escorts followed them in and inflicted heavy and lasting damage to the oil refinery itself. Japanese defences proved more alert, but the few interceptors they managed to get airborne were quickly engaged in combat and disposed of. We lost one aircraft, but the pilot was safely picked up out of the sea.

The Japanese had frequently broadcast their intentions to kill any captured pilots and the chances of being forced down either en route to or on return from the target area were daunting to the young pilots. Like the Americans, the Royal Navy endeavoured to pick them up if they ditched in the sea and destroyers quickly became highly efficient at this. The risk of being forced to crashland in the endless jungle wastes of Sumatra was a hazard they just had to accept.

The fleet returned to Trincomalee for the last time a few days later. All was now ready for the final passage to Fremantle and then on to Sydney. It was not expected that the enemy would dispute their passage in any way so it was proposed, following a request by Admiral Nimitz, to use the opportunity to throw one last punch at the enemy in Sumatra in an endeavour to knock out his chief oil reserves for the defenders of the Philippines.

The American authorities were becoming increasingly alarmed at the high casualty rate being inflicted by the Japanese suicide bombers and hoped that such a strike, if successful, would reduce the sortie rate of the enemy.

The BPF readily agreed to this suggestion as it was felt that they had by this time sufficiently overcome teething troubles and were ready to operate a larger force than hitherto attempted.

We were pleased with the performance of our American type aircraft [Admiral Vian wrote]. Their robustness, reliability and long endurance showed up in marked contrast to our own types, particularly the Seafires, which still formed the main outfit of the *Indefatigable*.

As well as American equipment we also adopted American ideas and techniques. A good example of this is the employment of Air Co-ordinators; their job is best described in official U.S. Navy parlance:

> This officer is an experienced and senior officer, usually a Group Commander. He patrols the battle area in his own aircraft, usually a single seater fighter . . .
>
> The Air Co-ordinator has to know in detail the plan of the operation and to be as familiar as possible with the terrain in which it is to take place. He is in communication by R/T with the Air Observers and the Support Aircraft Commander in the Head-quarters Ship . . .
>
> The value of the Air Co-ordinator is evidenced particularly during the most fluid stages of the assault. He can readjust the planned air support, and divert an attack to a different target when necessary. Flights of aircraft are constantly in the air, on call for bombing and strafing missions, and can be allotted their missions by the Support Aircraft Commander, usually through the Air Co-ordinator. This system is similar to the 'Cab-rank' system. The Air Co-ordinator is the agent in the air of the Support Aircraft Commander, and whilst the latter has the final decision on the allotment of ground targets to air attack the Air Co-ordinator is often called on to co-ordinate or divert the actual support missions, as he is in the best position to see how the battle is developing.

And now everyone was keen to get on with the job and press on into the Pacific to make their contribution to the final defeat of Japan.

5

Palembang

Once the decision had been taken that a British attack should
be launched against a key Japanese-held installation, the actual
choice was easy. There were two major oil complexes in the
Palembang area which up till now had not been molested by
the Allies. The East Indies Fleet had been fully occupied learning
its trade and building up its strength; the Australians and General
MacArthur's forces had been preoccupied with clearing the
Japanese threat from New Guinea; and the United States Fleet
was locked in bloody combat in the Central Pacific.

The first target was at Songei Gerong and had been the main
East Indies refinery for Standard Oil. The other was at Pladjoe
and near enough to be considered as a joint target; it was the
former Royal Dutch Shell site and was even bigger than Songei
Gerong. Taken together, the two refineries were perhaps the
most valuable target in the East Indies; between them they produced an estimated fifty per cent of all the oil used by Japan,
including about seventy-five per cent of her vital aviation spirit. A
heavy blow here would cause the Japanese irretrievable
damage.

It would obviously be too optimistic to expect to achieve complete destruction of the sites, but by concentrating on the more
vital installations such as the distilleries and refining plants output
could be very severely reduced for a long period, and this kind of
damage, at a time when Japan was suffering from increasing fuel
shortages and was facing renewed Allied offensives on all fronts,
could be decisive. The refining installations at Palembang obvi-
ated the need for much wasteful transport of the crude oil products
to homeland Japan for refining there. While Japan had facilities
to refine oil, she was by this stage of the war suffering from a
critical shortage of suitable oil tankers; many of these valuable

vessels had been lost to her through the devastating submarine campaign still being waged by the Americans.

If the target presented to us at Palembang seemed of such importance, the same point had not escaped the Japanese. Besides numerous heavy and light AA defences dispersed around both refineries, there were several airfields in the vicinity of Palembang town: Palembang airstrip itself; Lembak; Talangbetoetoe; and a small strip at Mana. We knew that the Japanese were using some of these airfields as training bases for all their Army fighter pilots in this theatre, and we could therefore expect some heavy opposition, particularly as it was thought that we would find a large number of instructors operating against us.

Apart from these defences, which were formidable enough, there was also the fact that the enemy now knew our methods. Once the initial surprise was over, we could expect a vigorous reaction. It was known that the Japanese had formed several squadrons of Special Attack Forces specifically to combat the Allied Task Forces. These consisted of medium bombers with crews specially trained to carry out low-level attacks on high-speed warship targets. This policy of specialised groups for such tasks had already shown its value to Japan's Axis partner: a special anti-shipping squadron of the Luftwaffe using Ju.88 bombers had scored some notable successes against the Royal Navy in the Mediterranean area.[1]

American sorties in the Central Pacific had not been met with much shore-based opposition, the initial American attacks usually having been of such density as to overwhelm the islands' defences; their most formidable opposition had come in every case from the Japanese Fleet's naval aircraft. But even so, the Special Attack Forces could present a serious threat and we therefore had to be prepared for the worst; as events turned out, these Attack Squadrons proved incapable of inflicting much damage on the well protected Task Forces, and the heavy losses suffered in skilled pilots was to hasten the adoption later of the suicide techniques for which training and skill were of less consequence.

Unknown to us, both refineries were protected by a balloon barrage. This was by no means a new hazard, the Fleet Air Arm pilots attacking Taranto had flown through one to sink three Italian battleships. But it was still very unpleasant to dive through

[1] For example this squadron had caught a British destroyer flotilla in the Central Mediterranean in mid-1942 and had sunk three out of four ships with such ease that it caused consternation among the Fleet.

a forest of steel cables, one of which could sheer a wing off a bomber with ease.

In order to allow for their passage to Australia on the completion of the operation the fleet had to make complicated calculations, in particular with regard to the fuel situation. The number of fleet auxiliaries at our disposal was still low and allowance had to be made for high speed steaming if a counter attack developed and also for any change in weather conditions which might necessitate alterations of plan and entail further time spent at sea.

The attack, code-named 'Meridian,' was preceded by a full-scale rehearsal with the fleet off Ceylon early in January. From this it was realized that our aircrews had much improved but were still not at peak performance. Nevertheless, it was decided that the force had just about reached the state of efficiency required to carry out the planned operation.

The first stage was set in motion with the despatch from Ceylon of the oiling force, the Royal Fleet Auxiliaries *Echodale*, *Wave King*, and *Empire Salvage* under the control of the senior officer aboard the destroyer *Urchin*. These vessels, designated Force 69, sailed on the 13th January at 1530 and were to be joined in the fuelling area south of Sumatra by the RFA *Arndale* which was to be sent from Fremantle on the 15th.

At 1430 on the 16th the main fleet left Trincomalee for the last time; it was code-named Force 63 for this operation and consisted of the 1st Aircraft Carrier Squadron, *Indomitable* (Flagship), *Illustrious*, *Indefatigable* and *Victorious*; the battleship *King George V*, flagship of Vice Admiral Rawlings; the cruisers *Argonaut*, *Black Prince* and *Euryalus*; and two destroyer flotillas, the 25th with Captain (D) in *Grenville* with *Undine*, *Ursa* and *Undaunted* and the 27th with Captain (D) in *Kempenfelt* with *Wakeful*, *Whirlwind*, *Wager* and *Whelp*. In addition the cruiser *Ceylon* was to join later with mail and likewise the destroyer *Wessex* with radar spares.

During the first three days of their passage to the fuelling rendezvous the fleet carried out night encounter, aircraft shadowing interception, destroyer torpedo attacks and various gunnery exercises to bring them up to full pitch and also during this time the cruiser and destroyer joined the force. At 0822 on the 20th the oiling force was located by aircraft of the fleet and between 0900 and 1850 the *King George V*, the cruisers and the destroyers refuelled. This was not made easier by frequent rain squalls and a fresh breeze which kicked up a moderate swell; some damage was

Corsairs in flight ▶
[Commander Hay

MERIDIAN I   [*Commander Hay*

Top: The attack on Pladjoe Oilfield from the Air Coordinator's aircraft. Note
the barrage balloons

Bottom: The Coordinator comes down for a closer look at Pladjoe   [*Commander Hay*

reported by the oilers caused by the destroyers which were rolling nastily. This showed how dependent our slender fleet train was on good conditions; with so little in reserve, the slightest mishap could cause delays.

On completion of oiling, the auxiliaries were detached under the protection of the *Ceylon* and *Urchin*, while the fleet steamed towards the distant enemy coast. The position chosen for the flying off of the strikes was coded as 'Position TA' and lay between Engano Island and the coast of southern Sumatra.

On arrival in this position during the night of the 21st/22nd, and again during the night of the 22nd/23rd, Force 63 ran into bad weather conditions and each time the start of operations was postponed twenty-four hours. An inter-tropical front with a belt of high winds and torrential rain combined to make flying out of the question, although it did perform the useful function of shielding the movements of the fleets from the prying eyes of the enemy.

The final approach was made on the night of the 23rd/24th January and the weather proved fine, the low cloud lifting so that by dawn the 11,000-foot mountain range over which our aircraft had to fly was clearly visible from thirty-five miles out. As the British Pacific Fleet was incapable of mounting two simultaneous strikes against both targets, it had been decided to attack each in turn and Pladjoe, being the largest, was assigned as first target.

Fighter Ramrods—groups of fighters whose job was to attack and destroy enemy fighter opposition on the ground—from this force were to cover the three main airfields. It was not expected that much opposition would come from the smaller Mana airstrip, but the *Indomitable* flew off a strike force of four Avengers and four Hellcats to cover it, just in case.

Illustrious and *Victorious* each contributed twelve Corsairs to form the Ramrods. *Indefatigable* used her Seafires, whose short range made them unsuitable for much else, to mount a permanent Combat Air Patrol over the fleet; their job was to keep away snoopers and deal with any enemy bombers should the Japanese Attack Forces put in an appearance. This duty they were to perform with great vigour and dash.

At 0615 on the 24th the combined striking force with its fighter escort started to fly off from a position about seventy miles east of Engano Island under clear blue skies. There was some delay in forming up, but at 0710 the force started on its way, the target being the key buildings of the Pladjoe refineries. Each Avenger was armed with four 500-pound bombs and the Fireflies carried rockets. The second range of aircraft, the strong fighter sweeps designed to neutralise the enemy airfields and the four bombers for Mana plus the Fireflies of the main striking force were then made ready. Again there was a delay in preparing the range and getting the aircraft airborne, partly because some aircraft of the first sortie were forced to return and carry out emergency landings. The second range was not fully airborne until 0720 and the Fireflies, despite going all out, did not catch up with the main strike force until that group had reached its deployment area. After crossing the mountain range, the strike force had a further hundred miles to fly in clear skies over enemy territory. Although the alarm must have been given as our aircraft crossed the coast, enemy reaction was slow. The Ramrod fighters overtook the main striking force on its outward journey and managed to catch the enemy at Lembak field completely by surprise; they destroyed some thirty-four planes on the ground. However, they were unable to prevent some enemy interceptors getting airborne from other fields and a fierce battle developed over the target area. At the Palembang and Talangbetoetoe airfields the fighter Ramrods found the enemy much more alert and the flak around the latter field was very fierce and accurate. Despite this, considerable damage was done and besides those destroyed many enemy planes were damaged or rendered unfit for combat, so that the main bombing force was unmolested until it was within fifteen miles of the target. The balloon barrage at 4,000 to 6,000 feet was an unexpected obstacle and individual pilots had to make their own snap judgments whether to attempt to penetrate it or to bomb above it.

About twenty Japanese fighters, Oscars and Tojos of the Army Air Force, managed to intercept but their standard of skill was low. Most of them were engaged and driven off by the fighter escort, but some made their interceptions as the bombers cleared the target area. The flak was heavy and accurate but all these hazards failed to deter the Avengers' strike-leader; he took his bomber down through the balloon barrage to carry out a pinpoint attack. Other bombers followed with the same gallantry and the main targets were devastated. Positions hit, as was confirmed from subsequent photographs, included a powerhouse, three crude oil distilleries and a refining unit. Two of our bombers were lost on the operation. Later reports confirmed that a cracking unit and the radio station had also been set ablaze.

Unfortunately, the course the bombers had to fly on pulling out of their dives took them over an intense concentration of flak which, unknown to us, was situated around the town of Palembang itself; some of the bombers were quite badly damaged by this, but all of them managed to reform at the rendezvous point and turn out to sea again.

The fighters in the meantime had broken up the enemy opposition and had succeeded in definitely despatching no less than thirteen of them, with a further six probables. The cost to our force was six Corsairs and one Hellcat; in addition to one Corsair and one Seafire which got into trouble and had to ditch near the fleet; both pilots were rescued unharmed. The small force despatched to Mana airfield found very little to occupy their attention. They dropped their bombs in the area, but claimed only one enemy plane destroyed on the ground. Subsequent Japanese broadcasts admitted the loss of fourteen planes but this figure probably did not include those destroyed on the runways.

A number of our damaged aircraft only just managed to stagger back to the fleet and ditch alongside the ships, but the destroyers were on their toes and as a result were able to pick up almost all the crews. We had also mounted a submarine patrol closer in, thus our pilots were always aware that salvation was near at hand if they could once gain the sea. Unfortunately, a few were unable to make it and their chances of eluding both death and capture were remote. A couple of Walrus amphibians were embarked in the fleet and on one occasion flew inland to Lake Ranan in search of a missing aircrew, but this was considered an extremely dangerous enterprise.

Sub-lieutenant Halliday piloted an Avenger on this raid:

We were all very well briefed on our objectives; we had studied photographs of the area and models constructed aboard the ship, and when we arrived over the plant the individual landmarks were easily identified. My own target, a cracking unit, stood out as a large cylindrical silver object. The type of attack chosen was really a cross between dive and glide bombing: it was the only way to neutralise a pinpoint target. It was essential to hit the cracking unit, and not just plant a bomb somewhere near to it. To achieve the right degree of accuracy we had practised this form of attack in our training. The bombs had to be released at a set height, using a sight, and if one veered from that at all then inaccuracies crept in and you would not hit the target. The main difficulty was that this was a fairly

well-defended target by any standards, and it is very difficult to
concentrate on your target when you know that people are firing
things at you—and the Japanese always used a large amount of
tracer to make sure that you could see something.

In other words one had one or two diversionary things to think
about, but once one started one's attack, everything else had to be
ignored; it was the pilot's job to hit the selected target on the
ground come what may and this we tried to do. It meant that the
bombers could not take any avoiding action, but must go in straight
and true, relying on our own fighters to keep the enemy off one's
tail.

There were three lines of defence which had to be penetrated
to reach the target: the fighters; the anti-aircraft barrage; and
finally a balloon barrage. This last was quite unexpected and
very effective.

The Japanese were very cunning in their use of the balloon
barrage. It was not floating at a set height, but they waited until we
were committed to our attack and then allowed the balloons to come
up. The balloons came up quite fast to meet you and in my opinion
this was deliberate Japanese policy and not because they were
caught by surprise. It was very well calculated to put a dive-bomber
pilot off. The pilot had to make a quick decision as to whether to
press home the attack through the balloons which meant flying below
the level at which they would be stabilised or attempt to pull up
above them.

Everyone quickly appreciated that if the attack was to be of any
use we would have to press on down, which we all did. We were
closing the target in a committed dive, so one was only left with two
options: you either dropped your bombs high, which immediately
meant that the accuracy would be very much less, or you went down
through the cables and dropped them at the right height. It is impossible, of course, for the pilot to see the cables, but one can see the
balloons and one knows that the cables are below though one does
not know exactly where. It is a very unpleasant experience, from the
point of view of a pilot, to be flying along one moment with an aircraft flying perfectly normally beside you—and then suddenly a
wing goes and the other plane spins down. We lost quite a few aircraft that day.

If one hit a cable very much outboard, you might survive; but one
could only afford to lose about two feet off the wingtip, striking anywhere else inboard of that towards the wing root and that was the
finish. The whole wing would go, and the plane would spin crazily
into the ground.

The fighter cover for the bombers was divided into two—the close cover and the high cover. The high cover's job was to keep the enemy interceptors away from the bombers altogether, but if they got through, then the close cover would take over. If an enemy fighter penetrated both covers and got through and behind a bomber, then that bomber was a dead duck.

The only protection the Avengers had was a ball turret, and the enemy did lose a few aircraft to these, because they were slightly incautious about attacking aircraft with these turrets—they probably had not come across them before.

I feel that this first raid on Palembang pointed to an enemy who was waiting, but was not as alert as he might have been. After all, it was a very obvious target and they must have been expecting a visit some time. They were well aware of our carriers operating in the Indian Ocean. The second attack certainly found the enemy very much more alert; they were waiting for us and we were intercepted much further out. Even in the brief time between the two raids, the enemy could easily deploy reserves in from other areas.

By 0940 the first planes started to land thankfully on the waiting carriers and by 1025 re-embarkation had been completed. The fleet then withdrew to the south-west at 22 knots. One enemy aircraft tailed our returning planes and possibly contacted the fleet; he was spotted too late for an interception, but even so he failed to follow our ships as they withdrew.

At 1415 a group of four or five enemy aircraft were picked up on the fleet radar screens as the ships were some forty-two miles south of Engano Island. Watch was kept on them as they circled the area, but they finally withdrew about a quarter of an hour later without gaining contact. The high combat air patrol which had been vectored out to intercept them was therefore withdrawn. No further attempts to approach the fleet were made by the Japanese. Nevertheless strict security was maintained in order to keep the enemy guessing as to our flying-off area and—to avoid any wireless transmitting—the destroyer *Ursa* was topped up with fuel and despatched independently on the 25th to the Cocos Islands with signals for despatch. *Ursa* rejoined the fleet during the refuelling period. This was carried out in two groups on the 26th and 27th, and the *Illustrious* and *Victorious* were topped up with aviation fuel at the same time. Again difficulty was encountered during refuelling owing to some of the buoyant hoses parting at the joints. It was not a good omen for the protracted operations for which they were training. Rear Admiral Vian had already reached the conclusion that the fuel situation would allow no more than one further attack. The estimated rate of fuel consumption, even at the comparatively slow cruising speed of 22 knots used throughout this operation, was found to have been a bit optimistic —and the Americans operated for a lot of the time at 30 knots or more.

While replenishment was carried out, the detailed reports of the aircrews were studied in order to learn how to approach the second strike. It was realised that the enemy would now be completely on the alert and was probably expecting another attack to complete the destruction of the remaining plant. Also, it was thought possible that some information might have been extracted from those taken prisoner—there were no illusions about the enemy's methods for gaining information.

It was not expected that the Japanese would be able greatly to reinforce their fighter strength in the area in such a short period, nor was it considered likely that they would be able to despatch any submarines from Singapore in time to cause us any concern. An alternative flying-off position had been arranged, but in the event was not used. There still remained the thorny problem of the heavy flak concentration encountered on the previous attack and the balloon barrage.

The counter measures decided upon fell into two main categories. First, the fighter sweeps were to be flown off in two parts, the timing of the flights being such that both groups, acting independently, should arrive simultaneously over both the main enemy airfields. In addition to ground-strafing runs, the squadrons were ordered to maintain standing patrols over these airfields to prevent the enemy reinforcing his combat interceptions.

Secondly, the bombers were instructed to turn right-handed immediately after completing their bombing runs and to proceed to a rendezvous south of the target area. This meant a longer withdrawal route, but was ordered at the specific request of the Avenger wing leaders in order to avoid the heavy anti-aircraft defences they had run into after dropping their bombs on the first attack.

As it was expected that the enemy would react strongly this time against the fleet itself it was further decided to strengthen the CAP at the expense of the fighter support over the target. To compensate for this somewhat it was decided to use the Fireflies as fighter support rather than as light bombers. At least four fighters from the other three carriers were to back up *Indefatigable's* Seafires.

With planning complete, Force 63 headed back into area TA at high speed on the night of the 28th/29th.

They arrived to find once more a belt of heavy rainstorms some thirty miles offshore. Not the least of Admiral Vian's troubles was the effect of a tropical downpour on the many aircraft parked on the decks of the carriers. Zero hour for take off was postponed from 0600 to 0640. At this time the fleet found itself in a clear patch between the storms, and clear skies were reported over Sumatra itself.

The striking force was hastily flown off for the attack on Songei Gerong, finally forming up for departure at 0732. The main strike was made up as follows:

Indomitable:	*Illustrious:*	*Victorious:*	*Indefatigable*
12 Avengers	12 Avengers	12 Avengers	12 Avengers
16 Hellcats	12 Corsairs	12 Corsairs	10 Fireflies

To cover Talangbetoetoe airfield *Victorious* despatched twelve Corsairs while two Fireflies were sent up from *Indefatigable* to carry out an armed reconnaissance of Mana airfield.

The deck handling parties' organisation had vastly improved from experience with the first mission and the time taken to prepare the second range of aircraft on this occasion was much better. As a result of this the Fireflies joined up with the main strike well before they crossed the coast and the fighter sweeps arrived over the targets on the dot.

As expected, the enemy had also improved and had standing air patrols already waiting before our fighter Ramrods arrived over their bases. Thus our pilots were deprived of any easy targets on the ground and did well to destroy four Japanese planes and to damage two others. Admiral Vian, however, considered that their presence certainly prevented the enemy rapidly reinforcing his interceptors, so that they performed a useful function.

The Japanese airborne forces were soon sighted and engaged in a succession of tough battles during which the losses on both sides were heavy. Despite all attempts our fighters failed to prevent a proportion of the enemy fighters from engaging our bombers as they finished their runs.

The new 'side step' route made the actual bombing manoeuvre more difficult but it was nevertheless successfully carried out before the bulk of the enemy defenders intervened. The exception to this was the unlucky 849 Squadron which had lost its fighter screen during the approach and was severely mauled on its run in. In addition it soon became apparent that the flak defences had been strengthened and that the standard of accuracy was far greater than in the previous assault. It was the leading squadron which bore the brunt of this formidable fire. As usual, despite the increased weight of the defence, the young pilots pressed in on their targets regardless of risk and all bombing was carried out with great accuracy. The balloon barrage was again ignored, many planes diving straight through it. Two Avengers paid the price for their daring and were shredded on the cables, including that of the wing leader, Lieutenant-Commander W. J. Mainprice.

Meantime the Fireflies attempted to destroy as much of the barrage as they could following this up with ground attacks on the flak positions. On the completion of their bombing run the surviving Avengers pulled up to reform for the long exposed flight back to the carriers. It was then that the bulk of enemy fighters pounced. 854 Squadron in particular was unsupported during this critical time and was severely harassed. Despite the lack of fighter support, no bombers were lost although a good many were badly shot up. They gave quite a good account of themselves; formation cover was not easy to maintain but individual bombers gave as good as they got. One Avenger pilot, Lieutenant (Air) G. J. Connolly, RNVR, managed to shoot down a Tojo fighter unsupported. This success was the result of typical selflessness. On pulling out of his dive-bombing run, he spotted one of his companions badly damaged and attracting enemy fighters because of his beat up condition; using his heavy bomber as a fighter, Connolly provided escort for his companion, not only shooting down one of the attackers but drawing off and thwarting several others. Happily the damaged Avenger managed to ditch near the fleet.

Sub-lieutenant Halliday was shot down on this second attack and he recalls the incident as a good example of how a pilot must concentrate on the target to the exclusion of everything else.

I was hit on my way down to the target, but I didn't realise it until I pulled away, and saw three or four neat holes in my wing and flames coming out of the holes. I just burned steadily all the way back to the coast—I did not expect to make it as it lay ninety miles away and on the far side of a mountain range. I was flying very low down when I was hit and realised that I would have to gain altitude to clear these mountains before I could reach 'friendly territory'. I had a lot of trouble: neither the wheels nor the flaps would lower, the hydraulics had gone, and the engine began playing up—it would only run, for some unknown reason, at a fantastically high rate of revs and every time I throttled back it threatened to stall and stop altogether. I just kept going as I was. I flew like this for half an hour with the wing blazing away like a torch and I cannot understand why it did not drop off miles back. Anyway, I reached the sea and to my intense relief saw a destroyer below me. I banked down past her, fired a Very light and pancaked close by her. She proved to be HMS *Whelp* and they had us all aboard in double quick time.

I could not possibly have deck-landed and it was just as well that I spotted the ship when I did. There was a submarine on patrol to rescue ditching aviators, but such were the casualties over the target that it rapidly became apparent that the situation was far beyond the capacity of one submarine.

It is amusing to note that by the time I was fished aboard the *Whelp*, a normal fleet destroyer with an officer complement of about six or seven, the rescued Fleet Air Arm officers she had picked up from the sea completely outnumbered them, there being eleven or twelve of us drying out in her wardroom by that time.

A fellow bomber pilot, Sub-Lieutenant W. Coster, RNVR, performed a similar feat when he was pounced on at low level by an enemy fighter. By skilful handling of his plane he managed to elude his opponent until the frustrated enemy had expended all his ammunition. The Japanese pilot then foolishly broke away in despair across Coster's nose. Coster promptly gave him the full benefit of his wing guns, resulting in a direct hit which sent him down in flames.

Another fine performance was that of Petty-Officer A. N. Taylor, a Telegraphist/Gunner in one of *Victorious's* bombers. His plane had been damaged by fighter attack before reaching the target, but his pilot had still gone ahead and attacked. Caught like so many others, just as they pulled out of their dive, they were heavily hit and the Observer was wounded. In between fending off several subsequent attacks with his turret guns, Taylor not only managed to administer morphia to the Observer and to apply a tourniquet to his leg but he also managed to use the wireless set to send out a distress signal when his pilot lost his directions. In addition he pinpointed the Avenger's exact position, told the pilot what course to steer, repaired the shot-up high frequency set and homed onto his carrier. As if this was not sufficient, when the damaged plane was unable to land aboard the *Victorious* after two attempts, and the pilot was forced to ditch alongside, Taylor managed to keep his wounded companion afloat until a destroyer picked them up.

The subsequent photo reconnaissance pictures showed just how devastating this attack had been. The whole area was a sea of flames and the bombs had fallen accurately into the target areas. An oil refinery is a difficult target to bomb successfully, representing as it does a very large area of separate installations with only a few vital ones scattered amongst them, but in this case the Fleet Air Arm made no mistake, extensive damage was inflicted on both the distilling and power-house complexes.

In his subsequent report Admiral Vian said he could not claim that full operational requirements had been carried out. But no target is simple enough to guarantee one hundred percent success and it is now known that the damage achieved was widespread and led to considerable curtailment of Japanese operations later in the war. It was not until Japan surrendered that the full extent of her fuel shortage was realised by the Allied command. The heavy damage inflicted on refining plant and distilleries by the young pilots of the embryo BPF contributed in full measure to this happy state of affairs.

The Palembang attacks were of immense value in increasing the efficiency of my young pilots in *Victorious* [Admiral Denny records]. I was always thankful for them because of the excellent training they provided. The real object of the creation of the carrier squadrons was for the final business of fighting the Japanese in their home waters, but it was fortunate that these earlier attacks took place when they did as the experience was first class and something we all needed.

Our casualties were not light. Altogether four Avengers, one Firefly and one Corsair were lost over the target and total loss through ditching and deck crashes amounted to twenty-five of all types. Against this could be set the heavy damage to the plants, thirty-eight enemy aircraft destroyed on the ground and thirty in combat, plus a further seven probables.

Our returning planes began landing on the carriers just after ten o'clock and an hour later recovery was completed. It was during these flying-on operations that the expected enemy counter-attacks materialised.

Up until 0900 the radar plot was clear of enemy suspects and the CAP patrols had nothing to occupy them, but at 0917 the Seafires spotted an enemy fighter which had probably contacted the fleet. It eluded the patrol by diving into cloud formations and it was not long before the position of our ships was known to the enemy ashore. Another enemy snooper was sighted at 0939. The Seafires quickly pounced and a Dinah was splashed twenty-eight miles west of the fleet. The ships were under cover of heavy cloud at the time and it was thought unlikely that this intruder had made contact. However, it seems likely that the fleet was spotted at this time as soon afterwards the enemy despatched one of his Special Attack squadrons. At 1026 this formation, twelve big twin-engined bombers, was reported closing the fleet from the north. The CAPs of Seafires and Corsairs were sent to intercept. Instead of the bombers, our Corsairs found two enemy fighters still apparently searching for the fleet and one was shot down; one of the Corsairs was also shot down. At the same time, several enemy bombers were detected about forty miles away steering south, having missed the ships. No fighters were sent against them as they were well clear.

Once again the screen went blank and the landing-on operations proceeded unhindered. When the last of the strike had been cleared down below decks the fleet began its withdrawal.

At 1152 enemy bombers reappeared from the south and again the Seafires were vectored out to engage. These aircraft were on a low patrol to the north of the fleet when first instructed to intercept and they were seen to engage the enemy just as the bombers were first sighted from the ships. The enemy formation consisted of seven bombers, one Helen and six Sallies and they broke up as the Seafires made their interception.

Avoiding the fighters they bore in to make very low-level runs at the carriers—*Illustrious* and *Indefatigable* seeming to be their targets. All ships opened fire with a heavy if somewhat erratic barrage and, through this, a further three Hellcats were scrambled from *Indomitable*. The enemy were at first thought to be torpedo-bombers as they came in at fifty feet and the ships manoeuvred accordingly. Despite the barrage the bombers closed the ships and a fierce mêlée resulted. During the confused fighting which followed every one of the enemy bombers was shot down without inflicting any damage on the fleet at all.

The Seafires splashed three and, assisted by the Hellcats and Corsairs, they are credited with knocking down another three; the ships' barrage accounting for the last. Unhappily, amid the wild firing, the *Illustrious* was hit by two 5.25-inch shells from one of the cruisers which resulted in the death of twelve men and injury to another twelve. Commenting on the lack of fire control afterwards, Admiral Vian stressed the vital need for this to be improved.

> It was [recalls Pat Chambers] not all that effective as retaliation, but it provided a fine spectacle from *Indefatigable* with burning and crashing Japanese aircraft all over the place and our fighters everywhere, regardless of anti-aircraft fire of all kinds from ships steaming at high speed.

The total annihilation of one of the enemy's much vaunted squadrons seemed to dampen his ardour. Between 1212 and 1430 the fleet was shadowed at a respectful distance of between forty and sixty miles but no further mass assault was forthcoming.

Just before sunset a lone Japanese plane, taking advantage of the fast dwindling light, was seen to edge in from the north-east and a CAP of Corsairs from *Victorious* was sent against him. They got to within three miles of him, but were vectored out too low and he was thus able to elude them. The patrol was then promptly recalled and finally completed landing-on twenty minutes after sunset. It must be remembered that the fleet at this stage had little or no night fighter capacity at all and was to remain without until the end. It was to prove yet another handicap when operating off the Japanese coast.

The lone enemy plane stooged around for another hour but contact with him was finally lost as the fleet withdrew at twenty-three knots to the west. Once he was shaken off the ships set course for the fuelling area.

The final stages of this remarkable operation were completed with the replenishment on the 30th. Refuelling was finished by 2200 that day and the fleet set course for Fremantle. Again to maintain secrecy, the *Ursa* was topped up with fuel and detached to the Cocos Islands, where she would transmit all necessary signals and then proceed independently to Fremantle. The final stages of the voyage passed without incident and Force 63 arrived at Fremantle at 0600 local time on the 4th February.

From Fremantle the fleet soon moved to Sydney where their base at Woolloomooloo was being prepared. At long last the Pacific fleet was in the Pacific.

The reception our ships received was gratifying. The Royal Navy was obviously welcome and the local population went out of their way to entertain the crews and make them feel at home, laying on shows, tours and suchlike and inviting large numbers of matelots into their homes.

The battleship *Howe*, having gone on ahead to Australia from Ceylon in December, had already experienced a warm-hearted reception, her crew describing their welcome as the 'Battle of Sydney', the whole thing had been so boisterous. It had been repeated in New Zealand the following month, when the *Howe*, escorted by the *Achilles*, *Queenborough*, *Quality* and *Quadrant* took Sir Bruce Fraser to Auckland and there is no doubt that the return of the White Ensign to the Far East was a long and eagerly awaited event. The Anzac press was quite lyrical. The *Sydney Morning Herald* said of the *Howe's* visit to that city:

> HMS *Howe*, flagship of the newly created British Pacific Fleet, was recently in Sydney harbour. Her presence was an official secret. During their stay officers and men of the battleship were entertained by Sydney people and they returned this hospitality by inviting their newly-made friends aboard their ship. An officer estimated the number of visitors as six hundred a day. The Captain granted passes liberally to his men, and everyone seemed proud to show Australia why the British Navy is still second to none.

While the *New Zealand Herald* added this to a report of a main battery shoot off Auckland:

> To be with the *Howe* and her men for even one day was an experience which will always be treasured.

All this enthusiasm was of course most encouraging for the embryo fleet but there were still many substantial difficulties to be overcome before they could rightly justify this praise. And the biggest problem still remained the Fleet Train.

6

'Iceberg'—Preparation

The United States Navy, with its vast resources, had by early 1945 perfected methods for all aspects of amphibious warfare and fleet supply on a grand scale. The Royal Navy had perforce developed smaller afloat logistic requirements and therefore had to somehow relate American practice to British availability.

The workings of a hypothetical Pacific operation, where the whole Fleet, sub-divided into Task Forces, might be at sea for a prolonged period, operating against a distant target, would fall into the following main stages.

The main bulk of the fighting fleet, comprising heavy and light fleet carriers; battleships; heavy, light and anti-aircraft cruisers; and destroyers would assemble at a Main Base where the ships would be fuelled and stored. This Main Base would be well to the rear of the fighting front and would be fully equipped with floating docks, storehouses and complete dockyard facilities. From here all big operations would start and here, while the fighting was carried on, would be assembled everything required for the developing situation in the form of spare aircraft and supplies. And here the main fleet with its auxiliaries would return before the next major push forward.

The Main Base selected for the BPF was of course Sydney, which was some 3,500 miles from Okinawa. Obviously ships could not withdraw between strikes over this distance and the next requirement was the establishment of an Advanced Base. Here would be located fuel and supplies, the more portable spares and some basic repair facilities. Here the fleet would call on its way to the target area to carry out final fuelling and storing before sailing at full combat readiness for the Operating Area. This Operating Area would be a square of ocean as near the target as would be reasonably safe from air strikes by the enemy—the tankers being very vulnerable to air attack. It would be identified by map grid references and given a code-name. From this rendezvous the Task Force would proceed to carry out its attacks and strikes, returning to it at two-day intervals to replenish before commencing the next stage of the attack. A fleet would be allocated several such areas and would choose the one most suitable with regard to weather conditions, resources and so on.

Between this Operating Area and the Advanced Base, the Commander of the Fleet Train would maintain a continuous shuttle service of replenishment groups, tankers, ammunition and store ships, escort-carriers with replacement aircraft, and so on. These ships, protected by their own escort vessels, would rendezvous in the area and supply the fleet's needs. They would usually include one or more escort-carriers operating fighter patrols in order to give the Task Force pilots a rest from CAP duties while replenishment was carried out.

They would also have their own anti-submarine screen of frigates and these would be in the charge of a senior officer, who was usually embarked in a destroyer.

The actual underway replenishment programme undertaken by these groups was extremely complex. On the conclusion of two days' striking at the target, the Task Force would withdraw overnight to the Operating Area to replenish. Contact with the refuelling group would usually be timed to occur at dawn. The support vessels would be strung out on a prearranged plan with their escorting frigates and sloops in a screen around them. The Task Force, with their greater speed, would approach from behind. The tankers and supply vessels of the group would be steaming in line abreast some six cables' lengths apart at the speed of the slowest vessel; their hoses and lifting gear would be all ready for transfer. To assist the foreign and merchant tankers—mostly Dutch or British—employed by the BPF, each had a Naval party embarked to assist in this function. The Americans commissioned their fleet supply ships as regular warships, thus eliminating time-wasting procedures. The Task Force would then reduce speed to maintain position with the replenishment force and their destroyers would co-operate with the latter force's escorts in forming one large defensive screen around the combined fleet. This period was always the danger point with all the ships of the fleet strung out and restricted to very slow speeds; fortunately the Japanese rarely, if ever, took advantage of these opportunities.

Once the screen was in position the maximum number of operational units would take up their replenishment positions. The larger vessels usually fuelled from astern the tankers, taking in buoyant hoses, although later the American system of abreast fuelling was used when a suitably fast, fully-equipped tanker belonging to the Admiralty, the *Olna*, was made available. The big fleet carriers would simultaneously take in a third hose for aviation spirit. The cruisers would fuel from alongside if possible and the destroyers almost always from this position. Actual fuelling capacity of the diverse tankers differed widely but an average figure of about three hundred tons an hour was usual. With a carrier astern and two or three destroyers or small cruisers taking turns alongside this still meant a period of up to eight hours had to be spent in fuelling, and frequent faults in the systems often entailed even longer periods.

Good station-keeping was an essential requirement during this tricky period and with some of the smaller replenishment ships used this was quite a feat.[1] When one ship had fuelled she would pull away and her place would be taken by the next. The first would then close another replenishment ship to embark stores or ammunition, provisions or mail. The destroyers would rejoin the screen while the larger ships man-oeuvred inside this protective shield to carry out individual gunnery exercises.

The destroyers would replenish in rotation and, in addition, would be called upon to carry out other duties including the transfer of personnel from one big ship to another; mail was transferred by heaving line, personnel and other equipment by means of a block and jackstay. A certain number of destroyers always had to be available to supply an adequate screen although enemy submarines were very infrequent visitors.

Ammunitioning the larger vessels had to be done by a whip and inhaul method with the supply ship operating the whip and the warship working the inhaul. The lack of suitably equipped supply ships was to be keenly felt by the British Task Force; in contrast the Americans had been able to build their ships specifically for this purpose and they were lavishly equipped with handling equipment. The hand-to-mouth methods we were forced to use quite understandably did not make a very favourable impression

---

[1] See, for example, *Sea Power* by Admiral B. B. Schofield (Batsford, 1967) for an amusing account of one such incident involving *King George V*.

MERIDIAN I   *[Commander Hay*

Close up of the target at Pladjoe

A Corsair landing-on with its drop tank ablaze   *[Commander Hay*

A Seafire crashes into the crowded deck park   *[Imperial War Museum*

on our Allies—nor did our employment of Lascars, Chinese and other non-combatant types in the front line.

One method which could be used to speed up the whole replenishing procedure was the refuelling of the smaller 'Dido' class cruisers and the destroyers from the carriers or battleships of the Task Force; this could be carried out at higher speeds—fifteen knots instead of eight when using the tankers—and most of this fuelling could be done whilst on the move from one combat zone to another, which was a great boon.

In the midst of this activity the escort carriers of the replenishment group would fly over fresh planes to the fleet carriers to replace those lost or damaged in the attacks, while 'flyable duds' were transferred back to the escort carriers for passage back to the Advanced Base for shore repair facilities. It usually took a full two days to replenish the whole Task Force complete, although every effort was made to improve on this. Whether in fact this could be done depended chiefly on the weather and the efficiency and capacity of the tankers and store ships provided.

On completion of replenishment the Task Force would then close its next selected target and carry out air strikes and bombardments throughout another two- or three-day period. The actual striking period would vary in length, according to various factors including the scale of enemy resistance, the success or otherwise of the attacks and the weather conditions, which in the Pacific area surrounding Japan included a season of frequent typhoons. At the end of each striking period the Task Force would again pull back to its Replenishment Area and repeat the programme as before with a new group up from the Advanced Base.

This alternative fuelling and attacking phase would continue for three to four weeks—the actual period being governed by the amount of damage suffered and the support received. When their stint was over the whole Task Group would once more return to the Advanced Base for major storing, repair and, in theory, a short rest for the crews. Any ships which were suffering from severe mechanical defects or battle damage would have their faults assessed and, if it was decided that they were beyond the repair capability of the Advanced Base, would have to be withdrawn to the Main Base. Their places were then taken in the front line by new ships fresh out from home waters.

This done, the reconstructed Task Force would sail as before to carry out a second period of strikes; usually the completion of this second period would be followed by the general withdrawal of the complete Task Force right back to Main Base for a complete over-haul and repairs before moving on to another target zone. The Americans could ensure that such a withdrawal of one Task Force would see its immediate replacement by another of equal size and power. The enormous size of the United States Fleet ensured that they could maintain at least four Task Forces, each of equal size to the whole British Pacific Fleet. They were always able to main-tain at least three of these off the target area while the fourth was away, and they could keep them on station for far longer periods than could the British. With only one British Task Force, its withdrawal meant the absence of any British force for several days between each sortie. In fact ships and facilities were being built up in Australia for the establishment of a second British Task Force, but the sudden ending of the Pacific war in August came before it was ever fully operational.

To keep the fighting ships within range of the target areas for the maximum period of time depended then to a large extent on the Fleet Train. To ensure and maintain the constant stream of supply vessels both to and from the combat area replenishment zone from the Advanced Bases, and also to keep a continuous flow of fresh fully-loaded vessels up from the Main Base to the Ad-vanced Base was the complicated task allotted to Admiral Fisher and his staff.

They had to ensure that everything required to keep the fighting ships at full readiness was always to hand when required: fuel oil and aviation spirit; bombs and fourteen-inch shells; razor blades and fresh food; everything. They had also to build up and main-tain repair units for every type of operation and be prepared to tackle modifications on anything from a 35,000-ton battleship to a Hellcat fighter.

The carrying out of all these functions required numerous specialised ships of varying design, size, speed and capacity, all of which in turn had to be convoyed, supplied and operated over the enormous areas of the Pacific. As we shall see, the British Pacific Fleet at no time achieved even the minimum numbers of vessels which it required. Those they did eventually assemble formed a dubious group, with a few notable exceptions, and included several foreign vessels without even the most rudimentary knowledge of naval operations and requirements. These were to work together with the more efficient vessels flying the Red Duster or Blue

Ensign, and somehow they all had to be worked up into a close-knit single unit.

Just to administer this Heath Robinson collection was a Herculean task, and that it succeeded at all was due primarily to the work and dedication of Rear Admiral Fisher, in command of the Fleet Train, and his large staff of regular and reserve officers. These operated from the various big depot ships which were maintained at each of the anchorages used by the fleet.

Admiral Denny, on the receiving end of the Fleet Train, has this to say:

> Afloat support was something which, in the Royal Navy, had been totally neglected before the war. Admiral Fisher made a terrific job of it; frankly, we all expected it to be an awful mess, but it wasn't, thanks to him and his staff. It was as near perfect as possible with what he had to use. It must have been a hell of a job—it had never been worked out before—but he did it.

The BPF established its Main Base at Sydney, with intermediate facilities at Manus and Advanced Bases were set up at Ulithi and Leyte.

An estimate of the minimum requirements for the Fleet Train listed the following:

7 Repair Ships.
1 Hull Repair Ship.
3 Escort Maintenance Ships.
2 Destroyer Depot Ships.
2 Submarine Depot Ships.
3 Aircraft Maintenance Ships.
6 Aircraft Repair Ships.
1 Motor Craft Maintenance Ship
1 Minesweeper Maintenance Ship.
2 Mine Issue Ships.
6 Accommodation Ships.
2 Armament Maintenance Ships.
6 Naval Store-Issuing Ships.
8 Naval Store Carriers.
10 Victualling Store Issue Ships.
3 Air Store Issue Ships.
19 Armament Store Ships.
2 Hospital Ships.
5 Fast Tankers.
2 Distilling Ships.
12 Boom Defence Ships.

In addition, a large number of smaller auxiliaries would be required, including demagnetising ships, small tankers, salvage ships, water tankers, colliers, floating docks, tugs, radio maintenance ships, harbour craft carriers and depot ships.

This estimate was drawn up in July 1943 with a view to supporting a Task Force consisting of four battleships, four fleet carriers, fifteen escort carriers, fifteen cruisers and fifty destroyers, as well as fifty escort vessels, twenty submarines, fifty Combined Operations ships plus landing-craft and minesweepers. It envisaged the fleet taking part in operations off the Philippines in 1944, so that when the operational area materialized much farther to the north many of the estimated figures became absurd, especially with regard to tanker requirements. Unfortunately, the effects of such a shift were not foreseen. However, this is a little academic as even the modest requirements listed above were never in fact achieved.[1]

It had been decided beforehand to use afloat facilities for everything that did not have to be ashore but there was a further complication; those facilities which did have to be established ashore were set up under the eye of the American authorities, and American standards differed from ours. Nevertheless, the Americans went out of their way to assist us in every way; this was a great help and sometimes vital to our success.

Requirements were worked out with the Fleet Train officer at each base on the arrival of the Task Force and he would meet them to the best of his resources and ability. Actual loading of supplies and stores was to prove as difficult as the afloat operations. Anchorages at the Advanced Bases usually proved to be at some distance from the supply facilities and the loading work all had to be done by the combat exhausted ships' crews. An acute shortage of small craft was soon felt for the transportation of supplies and this, added to the humidity of the area, meant that in effect, instead of a brief interval of rest between operations, the crews of the warships and the supply base laboured on without rest.

To try and understand why our forces were operating on a

[1] It must be emphasised that this original estimate was not rigidly adhered to, but was frequently changed in the light of operational experience. However, the acute shortage of shipping, coupled with the distance sinvolved from the United Kingdom to the battle zone, did make life very difficult for the British Fleet. Had the war in the Pacific continued beyond September 1945 the fleet would have been far more evenly balanced. For details of the Fleet Train as it actually stood on VJ-day see Appendix II.

shoe-string, we must briefly examine the history of the Royal Navy's afloat support capability as related to the BPF.

It was the loss of most of our main bases which first brought about a major reappraisal of seaborne support, but, owing to circumstances already touched on, nothing could be done at the time. The Admiralty drew up the list of requirements tabulated overleaf, in July 1943, when it was first thought desirable to send a strong British Fleet east. The list was made available at the Quebec Conference and, at first, the Americans were enthusiastic about the whole idea. As the bulk of the vessels required were merchantmen three organisations were involved in addition to the Admiralty. The first was the Ministry of War transport, which was responsible for maintaining the vital inflow of food and raw materials not only to enable this nation to survive but to carry out war operations overseas; this brought in the War Office who also had demands on available tonnage for the transportation of its vast armies and follow up material on a world-wide scale; and as the bulk of the merchant shipping comprised the mass-produced cargo ships of the 'Liberty' and 'Victory' types built in their hundreds in American yards and allocated to Britain under total tonnage requirements, after the United States Maritime requirements and those of the United States Navy were met, the Americans also had to be consulted and new ratios agreed upon.

The Americans knew just how essential these vessels were to maintain a fleet in the Pacific from their own experiences, but the two British organisations, in particular the Ministry of War Transport, failed to comprehend the magnitude of the task and were doubtful about the number of ships required and, indeed, about the feasibility of the whole scheme for seaborne replenishment. The Admiralty were in no doubt as to the urgent need for the ships, although it was later realised that their original estimates were out in allowing for too many depot ships and far too few tankers. The Admiralty was severely hamstrung in its attempts to convince these organisations by the fact that for a long while no hard and fast commitment was in fact made, nor was any specific date agreed upon for the actual despatch of such a fleet, until 1944. The vacillations of some of the American views of the desirability of our presence did not help their case and it was found necessary to despatch whatever shipping was available and hope that by the time the fleet was ready for operations the shipping would be available; not a very firm foundation on which to base such a huge operation.

The British mission to the United States reported back in early 1944 that the Americans would assist us in every way possible, but that our fleet would have to have its own supply arrangements and be as self-supporting as possible. It was felt that the American scale of logistics was very lavish, but even allowing for a more spartan British approach it was still found necessary to place the Royal Navy's requirements at 134 ships amounting to one and a half million tons, about two-thirds of which would be required for the Pacific and the remainder for the Indian Ocean. By March 1944 this estimate had been increased to 158 ships due to the increasing distance from Sydney to the front line.

The reaction from the Ministry of War Transport was that it considered that this would have serious effects on Britain's import needs, and it was suggested that as the Admiralty had already requisitioned more than two million tons of merchant shipping it should draw heavily on this 'reserve' rather than make further encroachments on new construction. This seeming deadlock was put before the Premier for arbitration and he specified the minimum imports into the British Isles at twenty-four million tons for 1944 and 1945 and stipulated that any further planning must conform to this requirement. This did not end the struggle, however, as the Ministry was still reluctant to release any shipping, and some American authorities were now vacillating about allocating ships they had initially earmarked for us.

Once the decision was taken to send the fleet out, however, the Admiralty doggedly overcame as much of this opposition as they could and as a result the fleet was able to operate once it was assembled, albeit on a reduced scale compared to its American counterparts.

Nobody was really right or wrong in this unhappy argument. There is no doubt that the supplies coming into this country did essentially have to have the number one priority and also that this lack of clear decisions regarding the formation of the BPF did seriously handicap any planning. The Ministry of War Transport seems to have failed to realise to what a vast extent naval operations in the Pacific relied on a Fleet Train; only Admiralty foresight in the gradual assembly of what few ships it had, enabled the fleet to become operational as soon as it did.

The basic reason why the Fleet Train was incomplete, however, was just the hard fact that after five years of war, during which the main enemy attacks had been directed against our Mercantile Marine, we just did not have the ships available—nor, by 1945, the crews to man and operate them.

In the end improvisation carried the day. Where there were no aircraft transports for the carrying of Fleet Air Arm aircraft, escort carriers were pressed into use, and so on. But nothing could make up for the lack of fast tankers and nothing did.

Fleet Train apart, before the BPF could join with its American allies in the war zone with any confidence, the new methods of fighting developed in the Pacific had to be learnt and tried out. And not only new tactics, a whole new vocabulary had to be assimilated. As the BPF was to become an integral part of the United States Fleet it was required to scrap its whole signals system and adopt the US methods. Everything had to be learnt from scratch, and the signals staffs had a full-time job on their hands with this vast reorganisation.

Strange new abbreviations became accepted language. A CAP was Combat Air Patrol, a standing force of fighter aircraft over the fleet; each ship was allocated a code name and the air waves were full of such phrases as *'Lucky'* and *'Tuxedo'* while more familiar RAF slang was intermingled with its American equivalents as: *'Six bandits, angels one, disappearing into ground wave.'* All Japanese planes were allocated boys' or girls' names according to types, and would be identified as a Betty, Jill, Dave, Zeke or Val.[1]

This knowledge was steadily assimilated but, as Admiral Vian wrote in his memoirs, 'none of us pretended to like it'.[2] The paper work involved in these and numerous other changes was recorded as of 'monstrous proportions'.

[1] See Glossary, page 202.
[2] *Action This Day*, by Admiral Vian: Muller, 1958.

7

'Iceberg'—The First Phase

Preparations for the 'Iceberg' assault were now at last completed. The islands round Okinawa were known to be heavily defended and it was plain that the enemy, now fighting on his own soil, would prove even more fanatical and difficult to dislodge than before. The position of Okinawa itself made aerial reinforcement easily possible, by flying in fresh planes either from Japan proper or from Formosa via the various island chains of the Amami Gunto and Sakishima Gunto groups; the enemy had constructed numerous airstrips in these two groups well defended by heavy concentrations of flak. To prevent such a flow of fresh aircraft through the Sakishima Gunto was the task allotted to the BPF.

Although it was fully realised that Okinawa would be a tough nut to crack, the enemy's strength in the event seems to have been underestimated.

The island had a standing garrison of some 75,000 men, well dug in behind elaborate concealed fortifications. As to the reaction of the Japanese Navy, it was known that they still had several battleships and cruisers operational and it was thought that these would be used in conjunction with the Kamikazes against the landing fleet. It was not known how badly crippled the Imperial Navy was through shortage of fuel; in fact, it was unable to sortie out in full strength.

Overwhelming sea power was to be employed by the Americans to crush this powerful bastion, supporting a total of four combat divisions—two Army and two Marine—with a further division held in reserve offshore. The great invasion Armada consisted of more than 1,200 ships, including a heavy bombardment group of ten old battleships, eight heavy and four light cruisers, with over eighty destroyers. Close-in air cover was to be provided by eighteen escort carriers and prior to D-Day air strikes were to be carried out by Vice-Admiral Mitscher's four Task Groups of the Fifth Fleet, operating as Task Force 58. These were to neutralise all enemy air opposition in Kyushu and to mount assaults on the enemy's Naval concentrations at Kure and Kobe. Task Force 57 was not employed in these opening moves as it was still assembling.

The American Task Force started operations on the 14th March, sailing on that date from Ulithi to strike at airfields in southern Japan. That the Okinawa operation would be no walk-over was soon realised when fierce counter attacks were mounted against the American Task Force, resulting in damage to the carriers *Intrepid* and *Enterprise* on the 18th. Despite this, the Americans inflicted heavy damage on the enemy without having their own massive strike capacity affected to any great degree; by the 23rd March Task Force 58 was launching heavy air raids against Okinawa itself.

The minesweepers of the American landing force commenced their work offshore on the 24th and the heavy bombarding ships closed to deliver the heaviest weight of shells yet thrown ashore. On the 26th the neighbouring island of Kerama Retto was captured and quickly converted into a repair base.

Meanwhile the ships of Task Force 57 had moved into position. On the 14th March the main body of the fleet, 1st Battle Squadron, 1st Aircraft Carrier Squadron, 4th Cruiser Squadron, 25th, 4th and 27th Destroyer Flotillas were at sea off Manus carrying out final exercises. The ships of the Fleet Train, Task Force 112, were in harbour at Manus, but only about a third of the intended support vessels had been assembled at this time. The following day they received orders from the C-in-C Pacific Fleet to report for duty, 'Operation Iceberg', to the C-in-C Pacific, Admiral Nimitz. All exercises were immediately cancelled and the main fleet put into Manus to fuel, store, ammunition and embark aircraft squadrons.

On the 16th they received a signal from Admiral Nimitz:

> The British Carrier Task Force and attached units will greatly increase our striking power and demonstrate our unity of purpose against Japan. The US Pacific Fleet welcomes you.

On the 17th, the two groups from the Fleet Train—or the Logistics Support Group—sailed from Manus so as to be in position for the opening of the assault. The first, designated Task Unit 112/2/1, consisted of the escort carrier *Striker*—with replacement aircraft—escorted by the *Crane*, the *Findhorn* and the destroyer *Whirlwind*. The second, designated Task Unit 112/2/5, consisted of the oilers *San Adolpho*, *San Ambrosio* and *Cedardale*; the escort carrier *Speaker*—for CAP duties—escorted by the sloop *Pheasant* and the flotilla leader *Kempenfelt*.

Next day, Task Force 57 sailed from Manus in the morning, arriving at Ulithi early on the 20th where they fuelled from American installations. Three days later Task Force 57 weighed anchor and headed north, finally to do battle in the waters of the ocean whose name they bore.

Task Force 57, although in size and power it was only the equivalent of one of Mitscher's four Groups which together comprised Task Force 58, was by British standards an imposing array. The ships which sailed from Ulithi at 0630 on the 23rd under the command of Admiral Rawlings, comprised the battleships *King George V*, flagship, and *Howe*; the fleet carriers *Indomitable*, flagship of Admiral Vian, *Victorious*, *Illustrious* and *Indefatigable*; the light cruisers *Swiftsure*, *Gambia*, *Black Prince*, *Argonaut* and *Euryalus*; the destroyers *Grenville*, *Ulster*, *Undine*, *Urania*, *Undaunted*, *Quickmatch*, *Quiberon*, *Queenborough*, *Quality*, *Whelp* and *Wager*.[1]

The main power of this force lay in its complement of aircraft embarked in the four carriers. At the start of the operation these totalled:

Indomitable:	*Victorious:*	*Indefatigable:*	*Illustrious:*
29 Hellcats	37 Corsairs	40 Seafires	36 Corsairs
15 Avengers	14 Avengers	20 Avengers	16 Avengers
	2 Walrus		

Of these the British Seafires had proved of too short endurance to be capable of much more than CAP duties, while the American types, sturdy and ideal for the work on hand, had been modified in several ways to suit British carriers which ruled out all chance of using interchangeable parts from our American ally's stock. With so little standardisation, flexibility of operations was much reduced, as each type had its own ranges, speeds and weight problem. In addition to the aircraft problems, our tankers of the Fleet Train

[1] Destroyer *Ursa* was docked at Manus; *Kempenfelt*, *Whirlwind*, and *Wessex* were with replenishment groups.

were generally smaller, slower and far less well equipped than their American equivalents, with the result that a great deal of time was wasted while the carriers were refuelled.

En-route to the fuelling area anti-aircraft gunnery exercises were carried out with United States Marauder squadrons providing the towing aircraft for the sleeve targets. Some over enthusiastic firing seems to have taken place which produced the following signal.

> From *Indomitable* to Rear Admiral Aircraft Carriers repeated to *Howe*:
> Regret two rounds of pom-pom fired in error in direction of *Howe* during test at 15.10 today.

Any hurt feelings aboard the battleship were no doubt countered by a message a few days later:

> From *Indomitable* to *Howe*:
> One of my aircraft handling party was struck painlessly on the buttock by a fragment of shell during Serial 5. Suggest this cancels my pom-pom assault.

> From *Howe* to *Indomitable*:
> Your 0950. Please convey my regrets to the rating and ask him to turn the other cheek.

In addition bombardment communication exercises were carried out by the two battleships and *Swiftsure* which suggested that the 'main ornaments' of the big ships would not be neglected. On completion of exercises the fleet formed up and proceeded at 18 knots.

In the early hours of the 25th the three small 'Dido' class cruisers were spread in line of search eight miles apart and eight miles ahead of the fleet to locate the Logistic Support Groups and make radar contact with them. Rendezvous was made at dawn, 0310, and the three cruisers followed by the destroyers were detached in turn to fuel. Here the first snags were encountered. It had been intended to complete fuelling by 1100, but a strong wind and swell coupled with hose failures made this quite impossible. The two battleships and the *Striker* were ordered to help fuel the destroyers, but even so the operation was not fully completed when it was halted at 1450. The carriers also topped up from the *Striker*, while a CAP patrol was provided by the *Speaker*. The destroyers *Quality* and *Whelp* both developed defects and were replaced by the *Kempenfelt* and *Whirlwind* from the replenishment groups. The

Wager was also left behind to complete fuelling when at 1530 the fleet worked up to 23 knots to reach the operating area by dawn.

The night passage was without incident save for a small fire aboard *Indefatigable* in the Carley floats under the island which was soon extinguished. *Wager* rejoined and at dawn CAPs and an ASP —Anti-Submarine Patrol—were flown off. The *Argonaut* and *Kempenfelt* were sent ahead for radar picket duty; this technique had been developed by the Americans to provide early warning against incoming raids and for this they used specially converted destroyers; however, the poor anti-aircraft defensive capabilities of our fleet destroyers meant that we had to use them in company with a cruiser in this exposed position, as picket ships were frequently singled out for special attention by the Kamikazes.

During flying operations we adopted the American practice of giving the Admiral Commanding the Aircraft Carriers tactical control of the fleet, as all movements had to defer to the needs and whims of the aircraft. Therefore at dawn Admiral Vian assumed control and at 0635 heavy fighter sweeps were flown off from a position one hundred miles and 180 degrees from Miyako Jima. Their targets were the airstrips at Ishigaki and Miyako, names soon to become all too familiar with the young pilots of the fleet.

Each island had three airstrips and it was the boring task of the fleet's bombers to keep these strips well cratered in order to deny their use to the enemy. It was dull work and very deadly for each strip was well protected by flak batteries which became progressively more accurate as the campaign wore on.

The initial fighter sweeps reported little or no activity on these airfields. They suffered one loss, a plane ditching twenty miles from Tarima Shima, but one of the Walrus amphibians was despatched and rescued the pilot without incident.

The fighter sweep was quickly followed up during the day by two escorted bomber strikes and a fighter-bomber strike; these left the enemy fields full of bomb holes and managed to destroy a few enemy planes on the ground. It was soon discovered, however, that the Japanese were managing to repair the cratered runways extremely quickly and also that they were very clever in the use of decoys to lure our planes down into their gunsights. This and the extensive use of camouflaged installations made accurate assessment of the damage achieved very difficult.

On the completion of these attacks at dusk, the fleet withdrew.

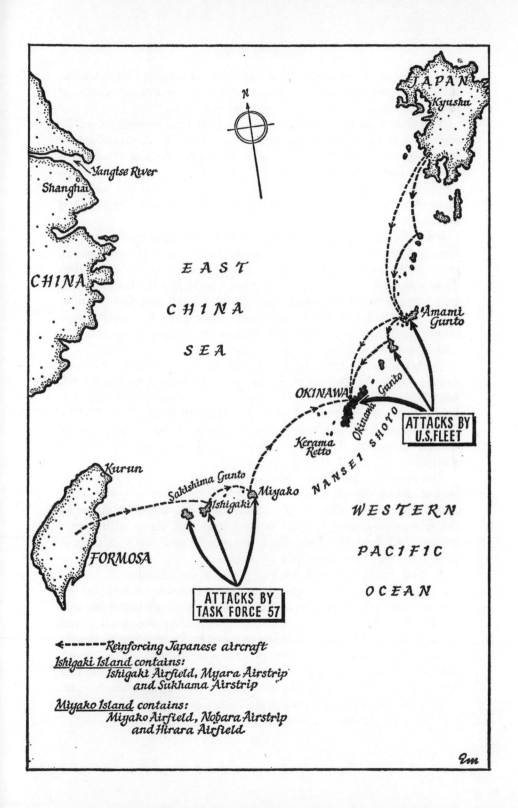

N

JAPAN
Kyushu

Yangtse River
Shanghai

CHINA

EAST

CHINA

SEA

Amami
Gunto

OKINAWA

ATTACKS BY
U.S. FLEET

Kerama
Retto

NANSEI SHOTO

Kurun

Sakishima Gunto

Miyako

WESTERN

Ishigaki

PACIFIC

FORMOSA

OCEAN

ATTACKS BY
TASK FORCE 57

←------Reinforcing Japanese aircraft
Ishigaki Island contains:
    Ishigaki Airfield, Myara Airstrip
    and Sukhama Airstrip

Miyako Island contains:
    Miyako Airfield, Nobara Airstrip
    and Hirara Airfield

Qm

The ships had been sighted early on by a patrolling Dinah which, although spotted, was not intercepted but the enemy made no attempt to molest the fleet throughout the 26th.

The fleet withdrew to the south-east in bright moonlight on the alert for a night attack. None developed, but the fleet was shadowed by one plane throughout the early hours and, despite receiving a severe shaking from the gunfire of the *Euryalus* and a near inter-ception by one of the fleet's Hellcats, reports that his airborne radar equipment was transmitting made it clear that he retained contact.

Before each dawn attack it was the custom for the two Air Group Commanders with the fleet to carry out a reconnaissance over the various enemy islands to decide on the choice of targets. This was also an American idea and, for the British Pacific Fleet, was carried out by Commander R. C. Hay,[1] and Commander N. S. Luard flying Hellcat fighters. Once they had made their choice and had reported back it was their task to co-ordinate and direct the strikes already sent out.

By dawn on the 27th the fleet had returned to within a hundred miles of Ishigaki and a fighter sweep was sent against the island, but they reported no outstanding activity. Again this was fol-lowed by two bomber strikes against installations untouched by the previous day's raids, while other Avengers had a go at some coastal shipping. The final strike was again a fighter bomber sweep.

Losses were again light; one of *Illustrious's* Avenger crews was picked up by the American Lifeguard submarine *Kingfish*, while another was spotted some 56 miles from the flying-off position by the destroyer *Undine*, having been despatched there with a pro-tective CAP from the fleet. She also rescued an American Corsair pilot who had been adrift for 48 hours.

It had been intended to carry out a bombardment by the battleships and cruisers against the main airfields on Ishigaki but this was cancelled when it was learnt that a typhoon was menacing the fuelling area; several ships were by this time low on oil, it was thought more essential to refuel, so as to be in position to launch further strikes during the period 31st March–2nd April, which was the time of the touch-down of the Okinawa assault forces. This decided, the fleet withdrew overnight to the replenishment area.

During the replenishment period their place was taken by the

[1] Actually, he was at this time Lt.-Col. Hay, Royal Marines.

American Amphibious Support Squadron of Admiral Blandy which kept up the pressure on the enemy.

At 'Area Midge', a rectangle of sea extending some 50 miles south by 100 miles west of a point 19 degrees 55' N 129 degrees 40' E, the fleet carried out refuelling and renewal of aircraft throughout the 28th–30th March. Replenishment was completed without incident by 1430 on the 30th. During this time Rear-Admiral (D), until then embarked aboard *Euryalus*, was transferred to the destroyer *Whirlwind*, which then returned to Leyte with *Striker* and *Crane* of the replenishment groups. The *Quality* and *Whelp* rejoined the fleet replacing *Kempenfelt* and *Whirlwind*. On completion the Task Force took their departure from the operational zone at 22 knots.

By early morning on the 31st the fleet was again on station and the *Argonaut* and *Wager* were detached for picket duties; the *Argonaut*, in particular, fitted with a superior type of American radar, was to guard against any enemy attempts to infiltrate our returning strikes with small numbers of bombers which could then carry out surprise Kamikaze attacks. Admiral Vian was concerned over the difficulty of distinguishing enemy aircraft, in the split-second time available, from our own. Both combatants' types of single-engined naval aircraft were similar, especially head-on, which is how one usually viewed a Kamikaze.

The dawn fighter sweep was despatched at 0630 but once more enemy air activity was slight. Throughout the day standing CAPs were maintained over Ishigaki and Miyako and bomber strikes were put in at these same airfields. Our losses were again light, another Avenger crew being picked up by the Lifeguard submarine *Kingfish*. This time when the fleet withdrew in the evening two fighters were held ready to intercept any snoopers but none were reported.

At 0600 on the 1st April the first American Marines waded ashore on the Okinawa beaches and initially found the going surprisingly easy. Under a hail of heavy shells and bombs they soon consolidated their wide beach-head. But afloat the enemy reacted strongly, Kamikaze attacks sinking two valuable ammunition ships during the first days.

On the 2nd April, however, the American assault was brought to a sharp halt by the Japanese holding prepared positions which had survived the massive bombardments. On this day, too, the enemy was stung into retaliating against Task Force 57, as they realised that it was menacing their supply routes up from the south.

The day started as usual; *Argonaut* and *Wager* were despatched to their picket positions and at 0640 the fighter raid was flown off. No sooner had the fighters taken their departure than bogeys[1] were reported on the radar plots to the west at 8,000 feet closing fast. At once the fighter sweep was recalled and vectored out to intercept while additional fighters were scrambled from the fleet. The incoming enemy split up while 40 miles out and, soon after, the CAP made interceptions. They succeeded in destroying four of the enemy, but others broke through and at 0705 the fleet went on to 'Flash Red' alert as the enemy aircraft commenced their dives.

The British fighters followed the enemy down in their attacks and caused considerable confusion among the fleet's AA defences which had difficulty in identifying friend from foe. One enemy Zeke made a strafing run over *Indomitable* spraying her flight deck and killing one rating and wounding two. He passed over the carrier and proceeded to machine gun the upperworks of the *King George V* from close range, without causing casualties. While the fleet was thus occupied another Japanese aircraft came in vertically, obviously in a suicide attack, and hit the *Indefatigable* at the base of the island killing four officers and ten ratings and wounding sixteen. The flight deck was put out of action temporarily, but was back in operation again within a very short time —to the amazement of the American Liaison Officers. Hits of this nature on the wooden-decked American carriers caused heavy casualties and enormous damage, usually necessitating the withdrawal of the ship for prolonged repairs. The armoured decks of the British ships enabled them to take more punishment than this and still carry on flying operations.

Lieutenant Commander Pat Chambers, the Flight Deck Officer aboard *Indefatigable*, had been hard at work since 0400 that morning, directing the strikes away: Avengers to carry out bombing missions and Seafires for CAP duties. One Seafire, piloted by Sub-Lieutenant Bill Gibson landed on with engine trouble and was struck down into the hangar for repair, after which there was a pause in the flightdeck activity. Commander Chambers took this short break as an opportunity to slip into the sick bay,

[1]Unidentified aircraft.

MERIDIAN II   [*Commander Hay*

The follow up raid on Songei Gerong. In the foreground a small ship has been
sunk by rocket fire

The destroyer *Ulster* after being near-missed by a bomb

The destroyer *Kempenfelt* refuelling from a tanker of the Fleet Train

located in the island structure, for a smoke and a chat with the assistant Medical Officer, Surgeon Lieutenant Vaughan, RCN, where he found Bill Gibson already installed. He describes the next few moments:

We heard a few bursts of fire from Bofors and Oerlikons from *King George V* close by us and as usual we started to put on flash gear and tin hats. Doc Vaughan was sitting on the sick bay couch and Bill Gibson standing next to me looking out of the scuttle. I was fully rigged for action with the exception of my left glove—I was just pulling it on, an action which turned me half to the left. This little turn was just as well for me, because at that moment there was the most shattering explosion and the sickbay disintegrated in a sheet of flame.

I was spun head over heels, over and over, or so it felt, until I got hold of a bit of jagged cornerpost, by which I heaved myself clear. In the steam and the din there was no sign of my two companions who had been laughing and joking a moment before. There was just a mass of dead and wounded in the area and one of my DLCO's, Sub-Lieutenant Peter Roome, helped me out onto the flightdeck and down a small ladder which led to a cabin flat. In one of these I passed out.

The picture I retain of the scene is quite vivid; the starboard wing of the Japanese plane burning on the island abaft the funnel and a great gap from there to the flightdeck where the whole lot had blown up, leaving a hole about eight feet long in the island sickbay. Our Kamikaze had had a bomb of about 250 pounds on him.

Pat Chambers was transferred, after a day or two, together with the other wounded, to the *Slinger* which transported them to Leyte Gulf where they joined the hospital ship *Oxfordshire* and later on the RNZN *Maungami*. He did not realise at that time that this was to be the start of three months' hospital treatment, recovering from blast burns and splinter wounds in the head, back and arm.

Luckily [he writes] we were to be well looked after in these ships and, later on, ashore at the Royal Naval Hospital at Sydney. Bit by bit our numbers were increased by the wounded from the *Formidable* and *Victorious*, and aboard the *Slinger* were also casualties from the *Indomitable*—one of *Indomitable's* casualties was my opposite number, Lieutenant Commander Chapman, who caught a bullet in the arm when the plane which struck us strafed her flightdeck.

Enemy planes continued to approach the fleet and our fighters constantly harried them, even through the fleet's barrage. During one such chase the destroyer *Ulster* was near-missed by a 500-pound bomb which opened her up abreast the funnel, causing the bulkhead between the engine-room and the after boiler room to collapse and flood both compartments. Two men were killed and one wounded by this bomb, but the ship seemed to remain steady. All power was lost but her guns were still active.

As soon as the raid was over the *Quiberon* was ordered to stand by her and the *Gambia* was detailed to tow her in to Leyte. After all top weight had been jettisoned, she was safely got into Leyte, and here the US Navy welded a plate over the 25-foot by 12-foot hole in her side. She returned to England under her own steam.[1]

Once this raid had died away a bomber strike was sent against Ishigaki but found it quiet. Following reports of further enemy activity at Hirara airfield, strikes were put in against this area and in the ensuing dogfight about fourteen enemy aircraft were destroyed on the ground and others damaged, though as to how many of these were dummies it is impossible to be certain.

Meanwhile the fleet continued to be harassed by occasional groups of hostile aircraft. A raid was intercepted at 1730 but was lost in cloud. Very soon afterwards, the enemy planes reappeared over the fleet and commenced their attacks. Again in the confusion several of our aircraft were heavily engaged by the ships' batteries while following hard on the heels of the attacking Japanese. A Kamikaze which broke through the defence dived on *Victorious* and only a hard turn under full helm saved her, the aircraft touching the deck with its wing tip and spinning into the sea alongside. The explosion left the carrier undamaged, though liberally cascaded with unidentifiable pieces of pilot and plane. Also blown aboard was a very interesting document listing the target priorities of the Kamikazes with carriers heading the list.

This air raid marked the final operation of the day and towards nightfall the fleet withdrew as usual to the south-east,

As it was thought that the enemy was now staging aircraft through the island airfields at first light to avoid our persistent attacks it was decided to cancel a planned heavy bombardment

[1] Where, at the time of writing (September 1968), she remains in service, being seen in the Solent throughout the summer, now reduced to a Frigate, but still active despite her 25 years.

and the normal bomber runs and, instead, to patrol over the airstrips at first light to catch them departing.

Indomitable therefore flew off two fighters to look over Ishigaki, flying off by moonlight; another similar sweep over Miyako was cancelled due to radio failures. However, nothing was found by the fighters and a later fighter Ramrod over this island produced only one Zeke, which was promptly despatched by the Hellcats. On the conclusion of this sortie the fleet withdrew for fuelling to 'Area Midge' the next day. The day's operations were marred by the loss of one man overboard from *Illustrious* who was never found.

Dawn on the 3rd April saw no sign of the fuelling force and the *Swiftsure*, *Argonaut* and *Euryalus* were sent ahead to locate them. By 0900 they had found them but by the time the fleet had formed up on the groups the weather and seas had become too heavy to enable fuelling to be carried out. The combined fleet stooged around the area throughout the day until reports indicated clearer conditions in 'Area Mosquito' further west. At dawn the following day further tankers arrived from Leyte making five in all and replenishment was started, continuing with many of the by now familiar difficulties until the evening of the 5th April. During this time a Task Group from the US Fleet took over their job of pounding Sakishima Gunto.

Despite all efforts, many of the larger ships were still only half fuelled when Admiral Rawlings disengaged and set course for the combat area once more; he took this decision reluctantly, in order to be on station as promised, and accepted the risk that possible battle damage might bring to a ship short of fuel.

The pre-dawn fighter sweeps were again launched from *Indomitable*, to cover Ishigaki and Miyako airfields but heavy cloud and little activity was all they could report. They also reported that all the bomb craters they had been at such pains to knock into the airstrips had all been made good in their absence; now they had to do the whole wearisome job all over again. Accordingly, raids were put in on Hirara, Nobara, Sukhama and Myara airstrips while the fighters beat up radio and radar stations and small coastal shipping, sinking three vessels. The Hellcats also despatched a Francis bomber after a thirty-mile chase.

Towards dusk a small enemy raid was picked up on its way in and the CAP intercepted, splashing one Judy. The other enemy aircraft broke through the cloud cover and approached the fleet. Two were hotly engaged by 4th Destroyer Flotilla out on the screen, both being hit and one coming down on fire; the other was finished off by the Corsairs and Hellcats of the CAP. A Judy was splashed by fighters ten miles out, but the last eluded them and made a dive on *Illustrious*.

The carrier took violent avoiding action and the Kamikaze pilot misjudged, one wing-tip struck the ship's island structure, tipping the plane into the sea alongside where it exploded. Captain Lambe on the bridge was missed by about nine feet by this plane, a fortunate escape. The plane would probably have struck square, the bridge being a favourite aiming point, had he not in fact been well hit on his final approach by the Bofors gunners. An unfortunate victim of the AA fire was a Seafire of the CAP, whose pilot was killed.

This small raid was the BPF's only taste of the 'Divine Wind' that day, but Task Force 58 to the north had been taking the full brunt. Over 700 planes had been sent against them, of which almost half were suicide planes; and despite receiving early warning the Americans were heavily hit. True, over three hundred enemy planes were shot down this day, but several destroyers out on picket duty were overwhelmed and sunk, while over twenty other ships were damaged.

Just as they were recovering from this massed assault, the Americans received warning of yet another assault on the way. An American submarine operating in the Bungo Strait reported a Japanese squadron steaming south at high speed. This turned out to be the huge battleship *Yamato*, her oil fuel tanks half-filled by borrowing from the rest of the fleet, on a one-way mission to destroy the transport fleet off Okinawa. She was escorted by the light cruiser *Yahagi* and eight destroyers.

They tried approaching by an indirect route, but their efforts were all in vain. At 8.20 on the 7th this powerful squadron was detected by patrolling planes from the US Task Force. At 10 a.m. a massive force of 380 torpedo and dive-bombers was sent against them. Despite heavy anti-aircraft fire—the enemy squadron had no air cover—the Japanese ships were simply overwhelmed by sheer weight of numbers. By 2.25 both the mighty battleship, the cruiser and four of the destroyers had all been sunk. It was a fitting revenge for the men of the United States fleet.

The despatch of the *Yamato* was followed with envy by the men of the BPF who had grown tired of their endless chore of cratering runways. Their attacks continued, however, and throughout the

7th they maintained constant CAPs over the enemy islands seeking targets to get their teeth into. In all, three bomber strikes were despatched to bomb Ishigaki, Hirara and Nobara all of which returned safely. In the afternoon the destroyer *Urania* out on picket duty with the cruiser *Argonaut* was despatched with an escort of two fighters to pick up a ditched Corsair pilot, but he was dead when found. It was unrewarding work for the young pilots, but it was also exhausting for other members of the team:

> The strain was telling on everybody now, and not the least upon the ship's batmen. The two of them, Cunningham and Johnny Hastings, slaved from early morning until late at night at their difficult and highly responsible job. Mentally they shared each cockpit, made every approach to the deck, their nerves pitching and falling in tune with the pilots own anxiety and fear of pranging in flames or drowning in a sinking plane. On one particular day Johnny Hastings 'batted on' sixty-one aircraft. It was not surprising if these two highly skilled, hard-working and conscientious men suffered as much from battle fatigue as the pilots. The Deck Landing Control Officer seldom received the credit he was due for this absolutely vital job—a job which did not end with his responsibility for the safe landing and take-off of the ship's aircraft, for the planes had always to be correctly 'spotted' on deck and that was a head-aching part of the job too. Before every take-off, fighters and bombers had to be spotted aft, dovetailed neatly together so that no confusion resulted when a strike subsequently left the deck. And when the planes returned and were eventually brought on to the deck, there was an additional headache, and backache, of arranging the deck park. *Illustrious* kept a permanent deck park for'd of fourteen aircraft, for which there was no room in the hangar. These had to be spotted and made secure. With the advent of the Divine Wind and the possibility of a Kamikaze crashing into these planes, all fuel had to be drained from their tanks each night. This hard chore kept the squadron ratings, the aircraft handling party and the Deck Landing Control Officers hard at it until nearly midnight—and got most of them up again at half-past three the next morning.
>
> And if it was difficult and tiring on deck, it was uncomfortable enough below. A pilot going to his plane when the ship was in the tropics dared not touch the metal, baked almost red-hot by the fierce sun, with his bare hands, but between decks it was if anything worse.[1]

Debits and Credits for the 7th were two Avengers lost by flak and four fighters from other causes; the enemy lost a total of

[1] From *Illustrious* by Kenneth Poolman: William Kimber, 1955.

three destroyed on the ground and four damaged, while hits were inflicted on several small ships around the islands. In the evening the fleet withdrew to 'Area Cootie' for replenishment, an American area made available to us as it was closer to our operating zone; US Task Force 52, took over from them as they pulled out.

Fuelling proceeded throughout the 8th and the cruisers *Uganda* and *Gambia*, and the destroyers *Urchin* and *Ursa*, rejoined after escorting *Ulster* to Leyte. The following day the destroyers *Undaunted* and *Whirlwind* were transferred to the fleet from the fuelling group while the *Whelp* was sent back to Leyte suffering from AS defects. The 6-inch gun cruisers carried out exercises while this was going on and fuelling was completed by 1530.

It had now become obvious that the more skilled pilots of the Japanese Navy had been flying direct from Formosa against the Americans off Okinawa, whereas those from Kyushu were generally little more than students. In view of the heavy losses being taken by Task Force 38 it was considered vital to interrupt the sorties from this source. The land-based air force under General Mac-Arthur's command proved ineffective, so the Americans requested Admiral Rawlings to take his force to perform this duty instead of returning once more to Sakishima. Although it was expected that the enemy around Formosa would prove more powerful, the chance was eagerly taken up by Task Force 57. On the 10th the fleet steamed to take up position 30 miles and 202 degrees from Yona-kumi Shima in readiness to strike at Matsuyama airfield. Heavy swell, fresh winds, low cloud base and drizzle met them and all flying operations were postponed until the following day.

Meanwhile the Americans were again hard-pressed. Throughout the 11th and 12th massed Kamikaze attacks were put in against them, the isolated picket destroyers again proving irresistible bait. The defending fighters and the barrage splashed hundreds of planes, but sufficient broke through to dash themselves against the warships. Two carriers, three battleships and fifteen destroyers were hit and damaged in this period.

On the 12th the weather had improved sufficiently to enable the BPF to begin to take off some of the pressure on their allies, but before they could launch any strikes enemy air raids began coming in and fierce aerial combat broke out around the fleet. At 0705 the Seafires intercepted four Zekes, destroying one, and ten minutes later the first British strike, consisting of two forces of twenty-four bombers and twenty fighters each were flown off. One force struck at Shinchiku airfield meeting heavy flak but no airborne interceptors. The other force met heavy weather over Matsuyama and so attacked Kiirun harbour instead, where they hit the dock area, a chemical plant and strafed shipping. Others bombed a railway station and factory while a bridge over the river south of Matsuyama was bombed. One Tess was destroyed on the ground at Matsuyama airstrip.

Meanwhile two Fireflies over Yonakumi Shima ran into a flight of light bombers and quickly despatched four Sonias and damaged another. The Corsairs destroyed a Sally on the ground on the same island and at 1135 others destroyed a shadowing Dinah. The enemy was everywhere. At 1410 a Dinah escorted by two fighters was intercepted but escaped into clouds, while an hour later Hellcats despatched a Zeke north-west of the fleet.

A major attack was sent against the fleet in the evening but was picked up and the intercepting CAP of Corsairs and Hellcats broke the enemy up before they reached the fleet, destroying one Val, five Oscars and two Tonys, our only loss being a damaged Hellcat which crashed on landing, killing the pilot. At the end of this successful day for our fighters, the fleet disengaged to the south-eastward.

Strikes were resumed at first light next morning, preceded by an impressive attack by four Vals. One of these aircraft in the half light made a dive-bombing run at the *Indomitable*, switching on his navigation lights and firing an incorrect recognition flare. Its bombs missed, but his daring paid off in that although heavily engaged he escaped unscathed. A second Val was not so fortunate and was destroyed by the fleet's barrage—as was also a Hellcat which had been flown off prior to the raid and failed to clear the area.

An hour later Corsairs splashed two Zekes 25 miles north-west of the fleet, driving some others away. At 0645 Avenger strikes were sent against Matsuyama and Shinchiku airfields, where they hit runways, barracks, petrol and ammunition dumps. The accompanying fighters destroyed twelve planes on the ground. The Fireflies destroyed a radar station at Yonakumi Shima with rockets and beat up small craft close by Iriizaki. On recovering the bombers, the fleet again withdrew south-east to replenish, the CAP patrol breaking up two further enemy attempts to reach the ships.

Commander Hay was as usual flying Air Co-ordinator for the strikes. He describes a typical mission which took place on the 13th April:

I was Air Group Leader for Strike *Baker* and our target was Matsuyama Airfield. We took departure at 0705 and as usual I flew ahead to report the weather. I made landfall at 0730; visibility was moderate but deteriorated rapidly over the hills and improved again towards the target. I therefore ordered the strike to fly round the coast and this they did, climbing to 8,000 feet. Unfortunately a solid layer of cloud built up over the airfield which prevented detailed examination of the target; the layer was 1,000 feet thick, cloud-base at 3,000 feet. I informed the Strike Leader of the conditions as he orbited overhead looking for a gap. He decided to bomb after diving through the cloud.

From down below I was able to observe the bombs striking the airfield until it was covered with brown smoke and dust. There was no flak before, but the moment the bombers appeared below 3,000 feet every gun went into action—they had evidently been waiting for us.

On withdrawal one Avenger bombed a factory and after recording the results by camera we strafed what was left. I also caught a passenger train which was skulking in a tunnel but which rather carelessly had left the engine sticking out. On the east coast my Numbers 3 and 4 shot up two junks and we all proceeded to Giran where approximately twelve aircraft of various types were spotted. One twin-engined plane was strafed but failed to burn.

Considering the weather I think the strike was a fine piece of work. There was no jamming and radio discipline was excellent. No enemy aircraft were seen airborne.

Because of the reports of heavy losses to the Americans during this operation it was decided that the BPF should try to maintain some pressure on the enemy and attacks were to be switched back again to Sakishima for the 16th and 17th.

It was late on the 13th that the news of the death of President Roosevelt was received.

At the fuelling rendezvous on the 14th they found the carrier *Formidable* up from Leyte with the destroyers *Kempenfelt* and *Wessex*. *Speaker* provided CAPs with her Hellcats while the force refuelled, and at 1755 the *Illustrious* was sent back to Leyte escorted by *Urania* and *Quality* to put right some serious defects.

The arrival of the *Formidable* was very welcome for, although her aircrews were as yet untried in combat, she had a full complement of aircraft which were badly needed if the BPF was to carry on attacking for another period; no aircraft replacements had been transferred during replenishment.

At 1400 on the 15th the fleet took departure for the combat zone, with colours half-masted as a mark of respect for the late President. Early on the 16th the fleet arrived off Sakishima once more.

For this operation, a shortage of fighters caused the abandonment of the picket ships and thus when at 0622 an enemy snooper was spotted he had ample time to get away before he could be intercepted. Two strikes were thrown against Ishigaki and successfully cratered the runways. A further two were similarly directed at Miyako and CAPs were maintained over both strips throughout the day. The Fireflies made rocket attacks on a radar station at Miyako. One amusing incident occurred at Miyako, when the Japanese called up our patrolling fighters and asked them to go back to their ships!

Between 1441 and 1730 numerous fast moving bogeys were reported in the vicinity of the fleet, but none came near enough to be intercepted. The Japanese at this time were using pilotless rocket-driven aircraft launched from bombers against the Americans and these sighting reports may have been instances of their use against the BPF. They were known by the Americans as *Bakas* —or Fools—because of their unreliability and certainly none of them got near enough to Task Force 57 to present a serious menace.

The CAP shot down a Myrt in the afternoon, but otherwise the ships were not approached—although several of our returning planes were reported as hostile and in some cases fired upon. The worst incident occurred when a Seafire landing aboard *Indefatigable*, bounced over the barrier demolishing an Avenger and a Firefly in the deck park and knocking two men overboard, one of whom was picked up by *Quiberon*, the other being lost. The pilot was unharmed.

Although shortage of fighters was acute, losses had been light and Admiral Vian informed Admiral Rawlings that he would be able to operate strikes for one more effort the following day. Admiral Rawlings concurred and informed the Commander, Fifth Fleet of his intentions. Thus dawn on the 17th found the weary fleet once more on station despatching further attacks against Miyako. Ishigaki was still unserviceable so was left un-attended. Three strikes in all were put into Miyako leaving the airfield unserviceable once more. A Walrus made a daring rescue a bare mile and half off Hirara town when an Avenger was forced to ditch.

There was very little enemy activity over the fleet; three Zekes were despatched during the day, while *King George V* put in some fancy sharp-shooting at a blazing drop tank ditched by a Corsair—it was mistaken for a Kamikaze. At 1945 the fleet withdrew for the last time in this phase of the operation and made for 'Area Mosquito' to refuel.

On the 18th and 19th replenishment was carried out and the *Undaunted, Napier, Norman* and *Nepal* joined the fleet. Mails, stores and correspondence was transfered but there were again no re-placement aircraft. At 1300 the fleet disengaged and the *Speaker* returned to Leyte with two frigates as escort while *Kempenfelt* remained in the area with the two tankers.

The final operation, on the 20th April, was a repeat of the earlier days, four strikes being sent against Ishigaki and Myako Islands, with standing CAPs and rocket attacks by the Fireflies. No enemy aerial opposition was encountered, though one Avenger had to ditch; the crew was picked up by an American Mariner. All the Japanese runways were out of action except for Hirara when the fleet pulled out at 1910 that evening. The whole fleet finally entered San Pedro Roads at Leyte at 1245 on the 23rd April after a month's continuous operations.

The hopes of those who expected relaxation and recreation were to prove illusory [Admiral Vian later wrote]. The ships lay miles from the shore, and the task of replenishing them with dry provisions and ammunition from the merchantmen, by means of ships' boats and such water-transport as the Americans generously provided, proved a day and night affair.

The huge San Pedro harbour, which had seen so much fighting, was divided between the Americans and the British. There were so many ships, the distances between them so great and night fell so quickly that boat crews had to be very careful not to lose their way or break down. One false step and your ship seemed to disappear completely into a darkened harbour. Coxswains were not to be envied at Leyte.[1]

[1] *Action This Day* by Admiral Sir Philip Vian: Muller, 1960

The Americans of course started sooner and finished later than our fleet but for a force operating under new conditions for the first time the BPF's first stint off Okinawa was very creditable. A total of fifty-nine aircraft had been lost from all causes, against which thirty enemy planes had been shot down in combat and ninety-seven, some of which may have been dummies, had been destroyed on the ground. It was not an awe-inspiring total, but was all that could be expected in such a war of attrition. All the American aircraft had stood up well to the protracted operations, but the Seafires had proved a constant headache.

Storing continued for eight days and then, on the 1st May at 0630 Task Force 57 once more put out to face the enemy, and this time they were to get a fight.

8

'Iceberg'—Fulfilment

Off Okinawa itself the US Fifth Fleet was still undergoing its ordeal by fire. On the 15th and 16th Mitscher went north with the fleet and launched a series of heavy raids on the airfields of Kyushu in an attempt to stamp out the nests of Kamikazes but although his pilots destroyed several hundred enemy aircraft there was no appreciable decrease in the scale of their attacks and several more ships were hard hit, including the carrier *Intrepid*. Of a total of thirty-three destroyers employed on picket duties six had been sunk and thirteen damaged; their sacrifice had prevented damage to the main fleet from being more serious than it was.

Despite renewed US attempts to throw back the Japanese defenders, a stalemate had developed ashore and casualties were mounting steeply. Fierce fighting was carried out from bunker to bunker, but no breakthrough was made until the 11th of May when the enemy were gradually cleared. The whole island was not secure until June, and the enemy kept up their resistance until they were dead; very few surrendered. Another tribulation was the launching of Kamikaze raids in massed formations at night. A few airstrips were working on the island itself and radar installations had been set up on offshore islets, but there was still no real solution to the suicide raids except a wall of fire from every available gun. Luckily, although the list of damaged ships was a long one, the Americans had available almost from the word go a repair base and this proved invaluable.

Even at this late stage the American Chiefs-of-Staff wanted to withdraw the BPF to the backwater area of Borneo, but Admiral Nimitz persuaded them to keep Task Force 57 in the main battle. On May 1st they sailed to attack Sakishima Gunto. The composition of Task Force 57 on this occasion was as follows: *King George V* and *Howe;* the carriers *Indomitable*, *Victorious*, *Formidable* and

Indefatigable; cruisers *Swiftsure, Uganda, Gambia, Euryalus* and *Black Prince*; destroyers *Grenville, Ursa, Undine, Urchin, Urania, Undaunted, Quilliam, Queenborough, Quiberon, Quickmatch, Quality, Kempenfelt, Whirlwind* and *Wessex*. For the initial stages of the operation, the 7th Destroyer flotilla, *Napier, Nepal, Nizam* and *Norman,* was assigned as escort for the Tanker Groups; the *Illustrious* was due to sail for Sydney with *Wager* and *Whelp* as escort; and the *Argonaut* was sent to Lae. *Ulster* was still at Leyte repairing. The lack of destroyers was still acute, enough being available for one screen, but there was nothing in reserve for emergency operations.

The fleet made rendezvous with the fuelling force in 'Mosquito Area' on the 3rd May and all the cruisers and destroyers topped up. *Uganda* fouled a propeller on a cast off oil hose, but was cut clear. By 1530 oiling was complete and the Task Force stood out for Sakishima.

The plans followed the usual pattern, but on this occasion it was decided to carry out surface bombardments to supplement the air strikes and prevent the enemy from carrying out repairs by night. The fleet was in position at dawn on the 4th and found the enemy waiting. Shortly after the first CAP was airborne the patrol intercepted a small incoming raid—shooting down one Zeke and dispersing the others. Two strikes were then despatched at 0605 and 0815 for Ishigaki and Miyako respectively. Runways, gun emplacements and dispersal points were all well hit, but increased AA fire was noticed. This further emphasised the need for ship bombardment to eliminate the guns.

While the bombers were over their targets, the enemy made repeated attempts to reach the fleet and probe its strength; their use of high-flying reconnaissance aircraft prevented our low-ceiling interceptors from reaching them and blind barrages from the heavy weapons proved equally ineffective. At 1000 Admiral Rawlings took the two battleships, the five cruisers and the 25th Destroyer Flotilla close in to the islands to carry out bombardments. This left the carriers with eight destroyers as screen and Admiral Vian arranged cruising formation so that two destroyers were equally spaced between each carrier to provide maximum defensive firepower and support.

About an hour after the heavy ships had left, four groups of Bogeys were detected closing the carriers, totalling some twenty aircraft. One group worked its way south, possibly acting as a decoy, and the CAP engaged them; a second group, however, eluded detection and surprised the defence. They were first sighted as they commenced their dives, and the lack of heavy anti-aircraft fire due to the absence of the big ships soon made itself apparent.

At 1131 the radar screens showed blank and then a Zeke was observed making a steep dive on *Formidable*. The carrier turned and twisted in a series of high speed wheels and fire was opened by every ship. The enemy machine was thrown out by the emergency turns and crossed *Formidable*'s deck at about fifty feet going very fast. He passed down the starboard side of the ship heavily engaged by all the close range weapons, banked hard over the starboard quarter where, once he got astern, fewer guns could be brought to bear. Before anything could be done, he dived at full speed into the flight deck abreast the island, releasing his bomb load just before he touched. The resulting explosions tore a trail of devastation through the deck park of aircraft, punched a hole two feet square in the flight deck, killed eight men and wounded a further forty-seven, and put all the radar sets save one out of action.

The flames and smoke engulfed the control positions and the bomb itself caused splinters which pierced the ship right through to the inner bottom and caused some damage to the centre boiler room.

Repair parties got to work at once to clear the burning aircraft and fight the fires. Even as they did so, at 1134 another Zeke broke through and made a run at *Indomitable*. She was at once joined by a second Zeke and both planes were heavily engaged by the fleet. The first was hit by gunfire a hundred feet from the ship and crashed into the sea; the second dived steeply at *Indomitable*'s starboard bow. The vessel was already turning to starboard and the helm was put hard over to increase the angle. Repeatedly hit by 20mm, 40mm and pom-pom shells, the aircraft slammed into the flight deck at a low angle and skidded across it over the side, smashing radar arrays and fittings as it did so. It finally exploded alongside without inflicting any very serious damage.

Meantime overhead the CAP had accounted for two more Zekes as they commenced their dives; both aircraft crashed in flames south of the fleet. No damage was inflicted by these planes. By 1254 the fires aboard *Formidable* were brought under control and she indicated that she could make 24 knots. The hole in the buckled flight deck was quickly filled in with steel plate and quick-drying cement. By 1700 she was able to recover 13 of her Corsairs.

Further incoming planes were detected throughout the afternoon and a Jill and a Val were despatched later in the day by the fighters.

While the carriers had thus been undergoing their most serious ordeal yet, the battleship force had formed up in open order, line ahead offshore from their targets; the three 6-inch cruisers were similarly disposed ahead of them; the two anti-aircraft cruisers inshore of them; and the 25th Flotilla screening to port. Conditions for bombardment were ideal and there were fighters overhead to act as spotters.

At 1205 the ships opened fire. The *Euryalus* and *Black Prince* using their 5.25-inch guns to carry out 'air burst' shoots on the AA positions around Nobara airfield, showering shrapnel down on the exposed guns' crews and decimating them. The *King George V* and *Howe* trained their mighty 14-inch barrels on Hirara airfield and the AA positions to the north. The *Swiftsure* and *Gambia* bombarded Nobara and the *Uganda* took on Sukhama. The bombardment was carried out as if on a firing range, with no opposition at all from the enemy. For fifty minutes the heavy shells smashed their way up and down the runways, ploughing huge gaps in the installations and parked aircraft; then at 1250 fire was ceased. A somewhat garbled message informing him of the damage to the *Formidable* reached Admiral Rawlings soon after the bombardment had started which caused him to break off the attack sooner than he had wished and rejoin the carriers at 25 knots. By 1420 the two squadrons had made contact and formed up in their usual cruising positions.

Photographs of *Howe's* targets proved that all rounds had fallen in the target area, and that all the airfields were thoroughly plastered. Morale among the crews of the heavy gun turrets was appreciably raised; now at last they felt they were pulling their weight.

The enemy continued to probe our defences, Corsairs from *Victorious* splashing a Judy around 1515 to the north, and at 1720 another Gestapo[1] Judy homed a group of Zekes onto the fleet. They were met by *Indefatigable's* Seafires who promptly despatched three out of the four Zekes plus the bomber without loss to themselves. A Hellcat returning from a CAP for an emergency landing was shot down by *Formidable's* gunners, understandably

[1] Gestapo: Code name for a reconnaisance-homing plane.

trigger-happy at the time, but the destroyer *Undaunted* rescued the pilot unharmed. *Victorious'* Corsairs destroyed yet another Zeke at 1820 during the withdrawal of the fleet to the south-eastward.

The following day, the 5th May found them on station once more operating somewhat reduced attacks against Miyako and Ishigaki. CAPs were maintained over the islands and three enemy planes destroyed on the ground and a petrol dump exploded. No flak was encountered at all over Miyako, a tribute to the heavy ships' shell-fire of the previous day, and it was hoped to repeat the treatment on the next attack date. This time, however, Admiral Rawlings intended leaving the two 5.25-inch cruisers with the carriers to strengthen their barrage while the battleships were absent.

Formidable continued her repairs, maintaining eight fighters at the ready to reinforce the CAP if required. By 0420 she reported that she was able to steam at full speed. Some of her Corsairs flying from *Victorious* splashed a high flying Zeke some eighty miles from the fleet from 30,000 feet. *Victorious* paid compliment to her 'paying guests from *Formidable*' for this splendid achievement; Lieutenant (A) Philip Clarke, RNVR and Sub-Lieutenant (A) Ian Stirling, RNZNR were the pilots responsible.

Commander Anthony Kimmins, RN, famous for his broadcasts on the work of the Royal Navy throughout the world, had been aboard *Indomitable* throughout this operation and now, loaded with detailed action reports of the Kamikaze attacks, he was flown to Kerama Retto with his press material in two Avengers with fighter escort. At 1905 the fleet withdrew to 'Area Cootie'.

Here they found, at 0630 on the 6th, the RFAs *Wave King*, *Wave Monarch*, *San Ambrosio*, *San Adolpho* and *Cedardale*, escorted by the destroyers *Napier*, *Norman* and *Nepal;* the escort carriers *Striker* and *Ruler* with spare aircraft for CAP duties; and the escort vessels *Crane*, *Avon*, *Whimbrel* and *Pheasant*.

While *Striker* replenished the air squadrons and the fleet topped up from the five tankers, the wounded from *Formidable* were transferred via the destroyer *Wessex* to the *Striker*. These wounded were later transferred to the hospital ship *Maungami* which Admiral Rawlings requested from Leyte. The Australian destroyer *Napier* relieved the *Kempenfelt*, which had defects, on the screen.

Replenishment continued throughout the 7th while US Task

THE BATTLE FOR OKINAWA   [*Commander Hay*
A strike goes in against Nobara airstrip, Miyako

THE KAMIKAZES

Top left: A Kamikaze hits the flight deck of *Victorious* and bounces over the side
Top right: *Victorious* seconds after the attack. She was operational again within
a few hours of the attack

Bottom: Indefatigable's flight deck after a Kamikaze had crashed into her bridge
island

[Commander Chambers

Force 52 covered Sakishima. During this day the news of the German unconditional surrender and the deaths of Hitler and Goebbels were received. The Task Force sailed for Sakishima at 1400.

It was planned to bomb the main islands and carry out CAPs as before; then to repeat the successful earlier bombardment, this time keeping the carrier group closer behind the battleship force to enable it to receive support quickly. But all such ideas were dashed when, on the morning of the 8th May, the weather worsened. The big ship programme was cancelled and four air strikes substituted instead. However, even this modest programme had to be abandoned as the weather got worse, with low cloud and rain squalls obscuring the target areas.

It was obvious that the enemy would be unable to stage through any aircraft to Okinawa under such conditions, so at 1050 the fleet withdrew to the south-east. If anything the conditions became grimmer as the day wore on but happily they improved during the night, so that the fleet was able to resume striking on the 9th.

Early morning CAPs over Hirara airfield reported that the field was again serviceable and so four strikes were sent against the islands during the day. All the airstrips were again well hit and left unserviceable, a direct hit being scored on one aircraft on the runway at Miyako. In addition the strikes hit barracks and a motor transport assembly area at Ishigaki. A more spectacular attack was carried out by the fighter CAP over this area. A Val was spotted hidden away inside a large cave and was destroyed by low-flying attacks firing into the cave with tracer; the secret hangar was left an inferno.

The fighting was not entirely one-sided, however. Enemy spotters were in contact with the fleet early in the day despite attempts by the Seafire CAP to keep them out of range. At 1645 Bogeys were picked up about twenty miles to the west. Their approach was fast and very low—typical Kamikaze technique— and they obviously meant business. The fleet went to 'Flash Red' alert and the CAP of Seafires already airborne was vectored out to intercept them.

One division of four Seafires nearest their line of approach intercepted at fifteen miles, but although they splashed one enemy the others broke through. Evading a second division of interceptors they rapidly approached the Task Force. Four of this group climbed to 3,000 feet and commenced their dives at about 1650. Admiral Vian had the fleet under full helm at 22 knots in a series of emergency turns, and all aircraft were heavily engaged by all the guns that could be brought to bear in the short time that the enemy was in range.

Admiral Denny was at that time Captain of the *Victorious*. He considered that the Kamikaze attacks were tactically extremely effective, 'a first class show from the enemy point of view'. He was fortunate in that *Victorious* was not the first carrier to be so attacked and he was thus better prepared to meet this form of assault. The only effective answer was to handle the ship correctly: by putting the rudder hard over and swinging the ship at the precise moment that the enemy pilot committed himself to attack. If the ship had full power available, and the timing was spot on, the aircraft would not have much time to correct and might have to start its run-in all over again. Usually, the Kamikazes would approach from the afterpart of the ship, from the stern or quarter, rather than from ahead or the bow; the trick was for the carrier to turn sharply towards his dive. If this manoeuvre was carried out successfully, the enemy pilot had no choice but to pull round and try again—but this gave the gunners more time to knock him down. Even if the Kamikaze managed to adjust his direction, a sudden alteration could spoil his aim and either lead to his over-shooting the target or hitting a less vulnerable point on the ship.

Victorious was the target of the leading two attackers. One minute after completing a 60-degree turn to starboard she was struck by the first attacker in a shallow ten-degree angle dive on the flight deck near the forward lift. The aircraft was heavily hit and well on fire before it struck, but the controls were evidently locked-on with the speed of the dive even though he was breaking up as he hit. The resulting bomb explosion and fire holed the flight deck, put a lift motor out of action and destroyed the catapult and one 4.5-inch gun turret. The fire-fighters immediately went into action and quickly brought the blaze under control, but as they did so the second Kamikaze was seen approaching also under heavy gunfire and well ablaze. This time the close-range weapons so hammered him as to deflect his power-dive from astern; burning fiercely the plane slid across the flight-deck destroying four Corsairs in the deck park, damaging a 40-mm gun director and some arrester wires, before it ended up in the sea alongside.

Our anti-aircraft fire was pretty effective [Admiral Denny records] and the *Victorious* was an immensely handy ship to handle, with a big rudder. I could spin her around quite rapidly and I managed to ruin both my Kamikaze attacks. They aimed originally for between the lifts—with American ships they could open up the flightdeck and go right through into the hangar space below; but eventually they found that this didn't work with the British carriers —they had armoured decks. Two Kamikazes successfully striking an American carrier could put her out of action with regard to operating aircraft but this did not work with the British carriers. This was possibly the reason why, later on, they seemed to go for the bridges of British ships with a view to killing the Command personnel—but this was a silly thing to do, because they could do far more by going for the hull of the ship. Damage to the actual lifts, while less spectacular, was a far more effective way of putting a carrier out of action.

The radar screen was effective but it was very difficult to distinguish a Kamikaze raid from a conventional one. This was another reason for the deadliness of the first run-in, it usually enjoyed an element of surprise, which was lost if the enemy was forced to make a second run-in. Even so, the first attack on *Victorious* was unpleasant, as Admiral Denny describes it.

Our first Kamikaze started from almost astern of us and my turn put him on my beam. He tried to pull up and start again, but he was not quick enough. I crossed ahead of him pretty close and his wheels touched the flight deck at right-angles. The undercarriage sheared right off and the plane broke up, sliding eighty feet across the flight deck to crash over the side and onto the 4.5-inch guns.

From the first moment I started to swing the ship, he had been trying to adjust and steer up the flight deck—which would have given him the whole length in which to drop his stick down and hit— but he didn't make it.

The Kamikaze pilots were good; they were not perturbed by flak—they had to be knocked down before they would give up. Admiral Denny confesses that he felt happier when he had a battleship astern, throwing up a massive barrage.

Sub-lieutenant Halliday was one of the pilots aboard *Victorious* and he experienced the first Kamikaze attack from a different standpoint to Admiral Denny—from that of the helpless spectator.

The Kamikazes always seemed to attack at a vulnerable moment, which aboard a carrier meant while the ship was committed to launching or recovering her aircraft. You are sitting, strapped in to the seat of your aircraft, on the flight deck awaiting take-off. Air Raid Warning Red is sounded: Kamikazes approaching. You can probably see them out of your cockpit. Everyone on the flight deck disappears to take cover, but you are left sitting in your aircraft and this is very unpleasant. The *Formidable* lost a large number of pilots and planes in this manner in one attack—a suicide pilot smashed straight into a deck park; a very effective attack on the Japanese part, but most unnerving from ours.

In this first attack the *Victorious* was hit on the gun turrets and it was the gunners who were wiped out, although the enemy usually aimed for the lifts where the carriers were most vulnerable.

From a ship, the only clue as to whether an attacking aircraft was a suicide plane was that the Kamikazes usually started their dives earlier than conventional bombers. If the Japanese had had more of them and used them more efficiently, the results could have been quite frightful. Admiral Denny, on the bridge of *Victorious*, was to have plenty of experience of Kamikaze attacks:

It is interesting to recall that each pilot would react differently; there appeared to be no set formula for an attack, other than the aiming point and the run-in. One could never tell whether one was up against a first class pilot or not, until the moment one swung the ship and watched the pilot's reactions. If one's timing was good, and the pilot was forced to re-think his attack, the majority of them would veer in at a lower angle which at once reduced their effectiveness if they did hit. If one could lead an enemy pilot to make a large alteration in his course, or if he failed to make an alteration at all, one felt secure that he would not score a hit. The fatal thing to do was for a carrier to steer a straight course, for in that case he would always get you.

In the cases where more than one aircraft approached, in all cases they would make separate attacks. One could watch them pick their targets, through a good pair of glasses, and as soon as the leading aircraft went into his dive, his wing-men would open up on either side of him for a different approach, hoping to hit you no matter which way you turned.

Total casualties from these two hits on the *Victorious* were three killed and nineteen wounded, but the ship was still able to operate aircraft after a short time. The damage to her lift was to prove a grave handicap, however, and much reduced her value on operations.

146

At 1657 the remaining two planes were observed making their runs against *Formidable*. The first was well hit by several ships as it approached and after making a pass astern at the carrier the pilot shifted target to the battleship *Howe* ahead of her. The much heavier firepower of the *Howe* cut the plane to shreds as it approached her starboard quarter in a shallow dive and after passing in flames over her quarterdeck the stricken plane plunged into the sea about one hundred yards clear of the battleship.

The fourth and last attacker was not deterred although likewise repeatedly hit by small calibre shells on his approach. Passing astern of the carrier and about a mile and a half from her, he suddenly banked to the left and headed towards the ship from fine on the vessel's starboard quarter, where very few of her guns could bear. Bits were seen flying off the plane's wings and body and then it struck the carrier heavily amidst the full deck park of aircraft and exploded.

The bursting of the bomb and the setting on fire and destruction of six Corsairs and one Avenger caused a great deal of smoke, but the bomb, which exploded some ten yards further aft than the previous hit, did not penetrate the flight deck. The *Formidable* reduced speed to fifteen knots to assist fire-fighting and by 1754 the fires were under control, enabling her to resume 22 knots. During the fire-fighting one hangar had to be sprayed, as burning petrol had penetrated it from the flight deck, and this caused the loss of a further four Avengers and fourteen Corsairs, thus reducing *Formidable*'s active complement of planes to four bombers and eleven fighters. One man was killed in this attack, the Petty Officer Gunlayer of the pom-pom mounting on the after flight deck who had gallantly continued to fire his gun until the plane struck a few feet from him; he was decapitated by an aircraft wheel.

The US Liaison Officer aboard the carrier gave it as his opinion that an American carrier struck in such a position would probably have been lost, but by 1755 both ships were able to operate although on a reduced scale. Admiral Vian then conferred with the C-in-C and they decided to withdraw to the south earlier than intended to sort out the damage. At 1950 the fleet set course for 'Area Cootie'. To balance our severe losses some eight enemy aircraft had been destroyed and several small craft off Ishigaki had been shot up.

These attacks finally sealed the fate of the 20-mm guns carried by our ships. All the attacking planes had been hard hit at long range, but these weapons had failed either to break them up, or divert them. Only the heavier calibre guns carried by the battleships proved capable of this and the need to install 40-mm Bofors aboard the carriers, cruisers and destroyers was given further emphasis.

During the replenishment period further tactics were worked out to provide the vulnerable carriers with better support during Kamikaze attacks. It was decided that despite the destroyer shortage the stationing of radar pickets—each consisting of a 6-inch-gun cruiser and a destroyer—should be resumed and they should be stationed at a greater distance from the fleet—twelve miles north-west and south-west. Each picket group would be provided with a permanent CAP of four fighters. It was also decided that the anti-aircraft cruisers should be brought in from the screen and stationed closer to the big ships where their 5.25-inch guns could provide a heavier barrage in their immediate vicinity.

The enemy's preference for attacking carriers over their sterns was to be countered by stationing a destroyer close behind each carrier during attacks to provide a concentration of fire against any further attempts to exploit the carriers' weak points. It was further decided to close the carriers up to a 2,000-yard circle to increase mutual gun support and to introduce a tighter formation for the protecting battleships and cruisers.

It was also stressed that the enemy planes must be brought under fire at longer ranges than hitherto achieved in order to deflect their aim. The coolness of the Kamikaze pilots in selecting their targets—some had been seen to make one pass, decide that their position was not satisfactory and go round again—indicated a high degree of skill and dedication among the pilots.

Early on the 10th the fuelling force was sighted, comprising the tankers *Arndale*, *Dingledale* and *San Amado* with the *Aase Maersk*, the carriers *Speaker* and *Ruler*, the tug *Weasel*, the *Whylla* and *Bal-Carat*, and the *Crane* and *Pheasant* under command of the Senior Officer aboard *Nepal*. Fuelling and replenishment of stores continued as usual; aircraft were flown aboard the carriers to make up their depleted squadrons; while Admiral Vian flew aboard the two damaged carriers to inspect the repairs. He was able to report that both ships were able to take part in the next planned series of strikes.

Fuelling was completed by 1640 on the 11th, when the fleet took its departure. The destroyer *Queenborough*, suffering from shaft vibration, was sent to join the replenishment group; her place was taken by the *Nepal*, and the *Kempenfelt* rejoined from Leyte, having completed her repairs. During their absence American Task Group 52/3 took over their duties off Sakishima.

Task Force 57 was back in position off Sakishima again by 0500 on the 12th, although this time they chose to launch attacks and recover from a position slightly further to seaward than the previous attacks. The radar pickets, *Swiftsure* and *Kempenfelt*, *Uganda* and *Wessex*, were stationed out at 315 degrees and 225 degrees respectively from the Task Force, and the destroyers allocated for counter-Kamikaze duty took station close astern of each of the carriers.

Under an overcast sky the first bomber strike was despatched twelve minutes after sunrise. As usual four strikes in all were mounted against the regular targets, but difficult weather conditions over the enemy positions forced the switching of one of the Ishigaki strikes against Miyako. All the runways at Ishigaki, Miyako and other strips were found to be serviceable and were well plastered again; it was like painting the Forth Bridge, but at least while the daily strikes continued the enemy could not stage planes through, no matter how diligently he repaired them every night. No aircraft activity was noted on any strip this day, but flak positions were strafed. One Hellcat was lost over Miyako during these operations.

On Miyako, the runways at Hirara and Nobara were cratered and attacks made on installations; three aircraft were destroyed on the ground, a direct hit was scored on a 4-inch battery and Hirara barracks and oil tanks were bombed out. Two Avengers were forced to ditch, but both crews were rescued; the first by the US submarine *Bluefish*, and the second by HMS *Kempenfelt*, led to the spot by the rescue plane from Kerama Retto.

No enemy aircraft approached the fleet and at 1930, after the CAP had landed on and the pickets had rejoined, the fleet withdrew.

The 13th repeated the activities of the 12th; once again the enemy failed to put in an appearance over the fleet and the usual strikes proceeded without undue retaliation from the air. Three attacks were put in against Miyako and one against Ishigaki. These struck runways, barracks, oil storage areas and shot up eight barges at Miyako. At Ishigaki storage dumps were blown up and radio stations left burning.

Around the fleet the first submarine alarms of the operation were sounded when at 0948 a possible underwater contact was obtained close to the fleet. A CAP of four Corsairs and three destroyers were detached to comb the area. At 1203 the contact was attacked with depth charges and Avengers joined the hunt, but although the hunt continued no substantial evidence of a positive contact was made.

An Avenger from *Formidable*, piloted by Lieutenant Philip Hughes, returned from a strike with only one wheel down, and unable to lower flaps. Because of his home carrier's damaged barriers it was decided not to risk further damage to her and he was ordered to land on *Indomitable*, which he did, making a perfect one-wheel landing.

At 1920 the fleet withdrew once more to 'Area Cootie' and Task Group 52/3 took over again. On the 14th the fuelling group was located as before, but CAPs had to be flown out to detect the second incoming group: *Striker*, *Wave King* and *Wave Monarch*, escorted by the destroyer *Nizam*. Forty tons of bombs were transferred by the *Black Prince* from the *Formidable* to the *Indefatigable* during the day, an indication of the time-wasting delays that could be caused by small items not being standardised; the American-type bombs were too large to be initially installed aboard *Indefatigable* at Leyte. Replenishment continued throughout the 15th.

It had been decided that the 25th May would mark the last day's operations by Task Force 57 against the enemy around Okinawa. The ships were due to pull back all the way to their Main Base in Australia so as to be ready for the new operations planned for July. This was agreed by Admiral Nimitz, as was also the fuelling of the *King George V* and three destroyers at Guam. Admiral Fraser offered to continue the British attacks after this date, providing losses remained light, but this was not considered necessary.

During the 15th the destroyers *Troubridge* and *Tenacious* joined the Task Force as did the *Nepal* from Task Unit 112/2/5. Captain (D) 25th Destroyer Flotilla, aboard *Grenville*, was left with the fuelling group and Captain (D) 4th Flotilla assumed overall command as Senior Officer Destroyers in order to give different Captains D experience in the job. The *Striker*, *Wave Monarch*,

Wave King, *Arndale* and *Dingledale*, escorted by *Napier*, *Nizam*, *Pheasant* and *Woodcock*, were sent back to Leyte in order that the Admiral Fleet Train would have sufficient ships at his disposal for the intended withdrawal later in the month. The destroyer *Nizam*, due to join Task Force 57, was kept in quarantine owing to some cases of infantile paralysis aboard; the Task Force disengaged from the tanker groups at 1705.

The fleet was in position for 'Iceberg 10' at 0510 on the 16th. Throughout the day strikes were sent out against their old targets, three to Miyako and two to Ishigaki, and all runways were torn up for the umpteenth time. Three planes were destroyed on the ground, a dozen small ships strafed and left sinking, a road convoy of troops was wiped out and five direct hits were scored on a large cave shelter. None of our aircraft was lost over the target.

During the day three of our planes came down in the water. An Avenger ditched while taking off from *Formidable*, the crew being picked up by the destroyer *Quality*; the *Tenacious* rescued a Corsair pilot who had been forced to ditch near the fleet after developing engine trouble at 20,000 feet; and at 1733 a further Corsair pilot came down some three miles offshore from Miyako—he was snatched from the unwelcome attentions of the Japanese by the Lifeguard submarine USS *Bluefish*, whose activities in connection with our strikes on the islands merited high praise in Admiral Rawlings' reports. No enemy were encountered in the air, either approaching or near the fleet.

Strikes were again mounted the following morning, but light winds were to handicap flying operations throughout the day. With two carriers less than one hundred percent operational, and defects appearing in a third, the *Indomitable*, it was considered best to reduce the number of strikes sent out and in the end only three were despatched on the 17th. The usual targets were well covered.

The *Victorious* suffered further damage when a Corsair crash-landed early in the morning, removing two arrester wires and both crash barriers, as well as dismantling three other aircraft as it passed over the side in flames, killing two men and injuring another four. Despite the rigging of jury barriers, the airborne planes from this ship had in the end to be accommodated aboard the other carriers, where they were parked on the flight decks, offering juicy targets to any prowling Kamikaze. Fortunately, no attack developed and *Victorious* was able to reaccommodate these exiles later in the afternoon. One Hellcat pilot had to bail out ahead of the fleet when the release button of his 500-pound bomb failed to function; he was safely picked up by *Troubridge*.

Replenishment was undertaken on the 18th and 19th in 'Area Cootie'. The fuelling force consisted of the RFA's *San Ambrosio*, *San Adolpho* and *Cedardale*, with the *Ruler*, *Chaser*, *Bendigo* and *Weasel* escorted by *Whimbrel*, *Parret*, and the destroyers *Norman* and *Grenville*. Again the *Black Prince* carried out the transfer of bombs between *Formidable* and *Indefatigable*, the small cruiser being by now quite proficient—she was achieving the rate of a bomb a minute. *Formidable* was disabled on the morning of the 18th by a serious accident when a Corsair in the hangar accidentally fired her guns into an Avenger struck down ahead of her. The bomber blew up and a fierce fire swept the hangar area. The fire safety curtains had been destroyed by enemy action earlier and the fire took a firm hold. The flames defied all attempts to extinguish them until the whole hangar had to be drenched with foamite. This catastrophe cost seven bombers and twenty-one Corsairs and left *Formidable* practically useless for strike work; she was reduced to flying CAPs and photo reconnaissance during the next attacks. In view of *Victorious's* defects with regard to landing-on aircraft, the decision was taken to keep *Formidable* with the fleet for the next attack in case of emergencies, to perform this duty if necessary.

On the 19th the ammunition ship *Robert Maersk* and the *Cairns* joined the group and bombs were transferred to *Victorious* and *Indomitable*. Poor weather reduced the number of replenishment planes flown over to *Formidable* from *Chaser*. The destroyer *Norman* joined the Task Force replacing *Nepal*. The Senior Officer Destroyers became Captain D 27th Flotilla aboard *Kempenfelt*.

The replenishment group was despatched to Manus while *Nepal* and *Parret* were sent to Leyte to reinforce the escorts for the Fleet Train. The fleet sailed at 1930 to take over from Task Group 52/1.

At dawn on the 20th they started to deploy as usual in readiness for the first strike of the day, the anti-Kamikaze destroyers closing astern of the carriers as previously planned. Soon after this manoeuvre commenced they unfortunately ran into heavy fog and the destroyer *Quilliam*, closing the *Indomitable*, collided heavily with the carrier. The *Indomitable* suffered only slight damage to her stern, but the destroyer was very badly knocked about, her bow crumbled up and was left hanging. By good fortune there were no casualties in either vessel. The *Quilliam* struggled clear of the formation and the *Norman* was ordered to take her in tow.

The fog cleared, but the weather remained poor with rain squalls and low cloud, so the C-in-C decided to remain with the cripple to provide her with support. In the meantime the Commander Logistics Support was asked to send the tug *Weasel* to take up the tow and the escort carrier *Ruler* to provide air cover. Meanwhile the *Norman* was having extreme difficulties in establishing and maintaining the tow; the damaged bow section acting as a rudder in the hard-over position. The *Black Prince* was despatched to have a try and by 1300 she had got the *Quilliam* under way at three knots.

The weather had lifted slightly, but only one strike was possible and this was despatched at 0745, reaching Hirara on Miyako with great difficulty due to weather conditions. Bombs were dropped on targets in the town itself and the Fireflies struck with rockets at likely positions in the island. It was a very unsatisfactory day and an evening strike against Ishigaki returned to the fleet without having located the target at all.

Over the fleet a few radar contacts were made but no enemy attack took place. Two Corsairs were lost; one hit by flak came down in the sea and despite searches was not located. Another went in after leaving *Formidable*, but fortunately the covering anti-Kamikaze destroyer rescued the pilot immediately. By 1845 the radar pickets were pulled back and soon afterwards the fleet withdrew southward.

The weather was still patchy on the 21st, but scout planes located clear areas and it was possible throughout the day to get airborne no less than five bomber strikes, three against Miyako and two to Ishigaki. Of enemy aircraft however there was little sign and the pilots had to content themselves with strafing and bombing targets of secondary importance as well as re-cratering the familiar airstrips at Nobara, Hirara, Ishigaki and Miyara. Cloud conditions made all attacks hazardous and difficult to evaluate.

During the earlier afternoon the Hellcats over the fleet intercepted and destroyed two Japanese snoopers but this was the sum total of the aerial activity for the day.

At dusk the fleet sailed to 'Area Cootie' where at 0700 on the 22nd they met the replenishment group, *Wave King, Wave*

Monarch, Aase Maersk, San Amado and *Robert Maersk*, escorted by the *Speaker, Napier, Chaser, Crane, Avon* and *Findhorn*. Also present in the area they found the *Quilliam* under tow by the *Weasel*, escorted by the *Black Prince, Ruler, Grenville* and *Norman*. As the British tug was proving equally as ineffective as had the cruiser and destroyer it was asked of C-in-C Fleet Train to despatch a larger vessel to get the damaged destroyer into Leyte and the Americans immediately made available their fleet tug the *Turkey. Quilliam* finally reached the anchorage on the 28th.

It was decided to send the *Formidable* back earlier than planned so that she could be made fully operational in time for the fleet's next major operation and at 1800 she was sailed to Manus escorted by *Kempenfelt* and *Whirlwind* both of which were in need of refits; their loss was offset by the arrival of two ships, *Termagant* from the newly arrived 24th Flotilla and *Quadrant* from the 4th Flotilla. *Grenville* replaced *Wessex* with the Task Force and commenced duties as SO Destroyers.

Replenishment was continued on the 23rd, and the Task Group was further reinforced by the cruiser *Achilles*. The day was marred by the loss, with their pilots, of two Hellcats from *Chaser*, and by the news that due to overheating on her centre shaft the *Indomitable* was reduced to 22 knots. That evening the reduced force took departure for the last time to the bleak waters off Sakishima Gunto.

Dawn on the 24th was again dull with drizzle, but strikes were launched during breaks in the weather and Miyako and Ishigaki were both well bombed, targets being the usual runways, a radio station, ammunition dumps, aircraft storage installations and two aircraft found on the ground by the Ishigaki CAP. These were poor returns and it seemed that the enemy had abandoned the area as a staging post now that Okinawa itself was almost completely overrun. None of our planes were lost during the day's attacks.

By the time 'Iceberg' was finished, the aircrews felt that they had proved themselves and that the carrier fleet was finally clicking at its peak. The old concepts of naval warfare had by then been finally rejected and the carrier was now accepted as the backbone of the fleet with the battleship as support. Operationally everything had run smoothly and, had the war run for a further six months, the BPF would certainly have come very much more to the forefront.

Even at the time of Okinawa, the Kamikazes had so reduced the strength of the American fleet carriers that it would only have been a matter of time—had the Japanese been able to keep up the pressure—before the British carriers with their armoured decks would have been hustled north to reinforce their allies.

> The operations in the Pacific [Commander Hay considers] were an entirely new concept of sea warfare to which our Naval leaders had to adjust with battles fought at two hundred miles' range, never seeing or hearing your enemy afloat.

It is to the credit of the BPF that they successfully made the adjustments, although in some respects they were still over cautious.

> For the first time in five years a British fleet was able to force its will on an enemy air force, but the spectres of Greece and Crete tended still to veil the fact that by 1945 the ships and planes of Task Force 57 were quite capable of taking on an island the size of Formosa—and could so do successfully. For the first time we had the strength, power and equipment to do this.[1]
>
> Of course, not everything was ideal. To crater the runways of the Sakishima Gunto was inevitably a long-term and boring job, but it was not made easier by the fact that the Avenger raids were carried out with 1,000-pound semi-armour-piercing bombs left over from attacks on the *Tirpitz*. What was the BPF doing in the Pacific with such weapons? They would have been of use had we been able to have a go at the *Yamato*, but there was not much chance of the Americans allowing us to have a go at her; for putting holes in runways, such bombs were of very little value. Then again, there was the shortage of rockets: although the RAF had been using them with great effect against ground targets since 1943 and the US Navy was also well equipped with them, they were virtually unheard of in the BPF. This meant that our bombers had to close their targets to much shorter ranges in order to destroy them than their American opposite numbers who could stand off at four times the range to do the same job.
>
> Once Admiral Vian was informed of this deficiency, he quickly moved heaven and earth to obtain more rockets, but it was then too late and only a fraction of our needs in this respect were ever supplied.

The final strike of the operation was carried out on the 25th May. The weather was again bad, but cleared early and three strikes hit Miyako, bombing runways, barracks, amphibious

[1] Commander Hay in a recorded interview, 1969.

bases, barges and the suicide-boat base at Sukhama. Ishigaki airfields were bombed for the last time and left cratered. One Corsair was lost, the destroyers rescuing the pilot. Again there was no airborne response from the enemy.

At 2200 Admiral Rawlings left with *King George V* escorted by the *Troubridge*, *Tenacious* and *Termagant* for Guam to consult with the Americans about the next employment of his fleet, while the rest of Task Force 57 withdrew to Manus. Thus came to the end the BPF's operations in connection with 'Iceberg' and the first real large scale operation by the Royal Navy against Japan since 1942.

> I would express to you, to your officers and to your men [Admiral Spruance signalled Task Force 57], after two months operating as a Fifth Fleet Task Force, my appreciation of your fine work and co-operative spirit. Task Force 57 has mirrored the great traditions of the Royal Navy to the American Task Forces.

In his report Admiral Sir Bruce Fraser stated that, in his opinion, the British Pacific Fleet had become 'not only welcome but necessary in Central Pacific operations'. It is only necessary to list their achievements to agree with his summing up. Since 'Iceberg' commenced the total was impressive:

Sorties flown:
Offensive—2,073.
Defensive—3,262.
Weight of material delivered against targets:
Bombs—958 tons.
Rockets—over 300.
Shells (14″, 6″ and 5.25″)—200 tons.
Enemy aircraft destroyed:
96 (all types).
Small craft destroyed:
200 (under 250 tons each).

Against this our losses were 98 aircraft on operations and a further 62 in accidents. The Task Force had been at sea for sixty-two days broken only by an eight-day restoring period at Leyte. For a first attempt it was a worthy record.

9

Interlude and Truk

Task Force 57 withdrew from the Okinawa campaign to refit at Sydney before the main operation had ended, but the final victory was not long to be delayed. On the 28th May Admiral Halsey took command of the American fleet and the Fifth Fleet became the Third Fleet once more, Admiral McCain taking over the Carrier Force from Admiral Mitscher. The composition of the Task Forces however remained the same.

Halsey continued the tactics of his predecessor and during the following weeks the Third Fleet moved north to strike heavily at enemy airfields on Kyushu. The scale of the enemy's resistance had notably been reduced after their last all-out effort between the 24th and 28th of May. Three hundred planes were shot down in attacks on the US fleet and only two ships lost. The Americans suffered far more severe damage on the 5th June when they were caught in the track of a typhoon while off Southern Japan. Thirty-six ships were damaged and some 150 aircraft written off.

Despite this setback, Halsey resumed his attacks on the Japanese mainland two days later.

On the island of Okinawa itself resistance was crumbling; although isolated units held out in the maze of fox-holes and interconnecting tunnels right until the Japanese surrender, by the end of June the island was effectively in American hands. Almost the entire Japanese garrison had been killed, while American losses were over 12,000 men. In the air, the Kamikazes had succeeded in inflicting severe damage to scores of Allied ships, but they had only sunk twenty-four and these were of minor types. Estimated Japanese aircraft losses reached a fantastic 7,800, while the Allied losses, including those for Task Force 57, totalled some 763 of all types over the same period. It was a resounding victory for Allied seapower and now the way to Japan proper lay open.

Meanwhile to the south General MacArthur continued to eject the Japanese from the islands and fortresses of the Philippines, following which it was decided to retake the north of Borneo with Australian forces. These operations commenced in June and continued successfully throughout the month, by which time Tarakan, Brunei, Seria and Mori were all occupied. Various cruisers and destroyers of the BPF assisted in covering these landings together with the RAN ships under MacArthur's command.

Next it was considered essential to recapture Balikpapan in Dutch Borneo, this being the richest oil centre in the Far East after Palembang which the BPF had virtually eliminated earlier in the year. Here the Japanese had constructed strong defences and guarded all seaward approaches with thick minefields. Heavy aerial bombardment throughout late June razed most of the oil tanks to the ground and caused widespread destruction in the area of the town. Cruisers and destroyers of the Australian Navy laid down a heavy bombardment in the week preceding the landings, while their minesweepers suffered losses preparing the way. The touchdown was on 1st July and although the troops quickly captured the town, enemy resistance in the hinterland continued until the end of the war.

While these conquests were in train, the BPF had dispersed to undergo refitting before commencing their next major effort. It was unfortunate that our ships had to withdraw 3,500 miles from Leyte to carry out such a refit, but even Sydney could not cope with the whole fleet and its attendant vessels; some cruisers and destroyers had to make do with what resources they could find at Manus, while the battleship *Howe* had to steam an additional 5,000 miles across the Indian Ocean to Durban. Such colossal mileages and enforced breaks away from the front line, which was now to move up towards Japan itself, were heartbreaking complications to those striving to focus the major effort of our fleet on to the final assault.

All four carriers were put in hand for battle damage repairs at once and fresh squadrons were embarked from the reserves slowly building up ashore. The *Indomitable* was found to be in need of a larger refit and it was considered doubtful if she would in fact be ready in time for the forthcoming operations. Further reinforcements were continually arriving from home waters and

158

A Japanese carrier under attack ▶
by aircraft of Task Force 57
[Imperial War Museum

The battleship *King George V* arriving at Guam   [*Imperial War Museum*

Admiral Fraser signing the Japanese Surrender. Behind him stand General
MacArthur, Admiral Rawlings and Admiral Brind   [*Admiral Fraser*

the *Implacable* had arrived earlier with some cruisers and destroyers.

These newly arrived vessels were considered to be in need of combat experience and a suitable target was found for them in the old Japanese main base of Truk in the Caroline Islands. Already isolated after the great American sweeps across the Central Pacific, it still contained heavy fortifications and resources which would provide more than adequate target material for the young pilots and also for the gun crews of the cruisers.

Implacable's crew, however, were in no doubt about their standard of readiness, blooded or not. Commander Lamb, at that time Flight Deck Officer aboard, recalls:

> When we arrived in the Pacific we held exercises with the other carriers, which had been out there some time, and it was expected that we would fall far short of Pacific operational requirements. In the event, we came through with flying colours; despite the fact that we had about ten more aircraft on our strength than the other carriers, we embarked and struck down all ours twenty minutes ahead of our nearest rival; on top of this, during a practice flight, all our bombers got through the CAPs put up by our opposite numbers. This was an auspicious start and Admiral Vian sent the signal: 'Proud to have you with us.'

Truk itself had already received severe poundings from both sea and air. On the 15th February 1943 Admiral Spruance had taken the Fast Carrier Task Force, consisting of nine carriers, six battleships and supporting cruisers and destroyers, to within one hundred miles of the base and had launched heavy air attacks against it. Taken completely by surprise, the Japanese lost over 230 aircraft which practically wiped out their air strength at the base. In addition, although the main fleet was absent, the American Navy pilots caught a cruiser squadron in the harbour and sank three cruisers, *Agano*, *Naka* and *Katori* plus four destroyers, and heavily damaged several others. In addition the Americans sank two auxiliary cruisers and twenty-four merchant ships in the ensuing bombardments by the heavy ships of the Task Force.

The Americans paid a very light price for this audacious attack right into the heart of the enemy's defensive zone, as it was at that time. The carrier *Intrepid* was damaged and a total of 45 planes were lost. This raid ended the use of Truk as the main forward

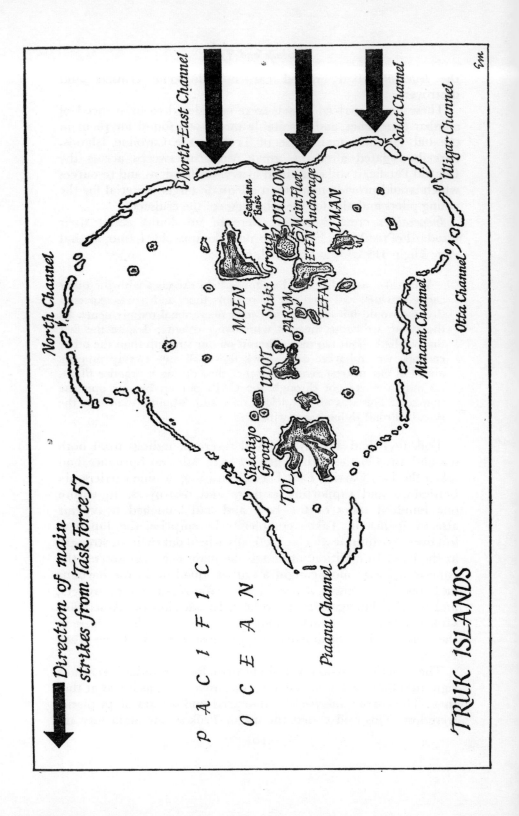

TRUK ISLANDS

Direction of main
strikes from Task Force 57

PACIFIC
OCEAN

North Channel

North-East Channel

Salat Channel

Uligar Channel

Seaplane
Base

DUBLON

Main Fleet

ETEN Anchorage

ULMAN

Shiki Group

MOEN

PARAM

FEFAN

UDOT

Shichiyo
Group

TOL

Minami Channel

Otta Channel

Paanu Channel

base for the Imperial Fleet, which then withdrew to the Philippines and Malaya.

As if this were not sufficient, the Americans repeated the performance the following April, when they again devastated the installations and harbour facilities, although shipping targets were then sparse. Since then the base had been isolated but still retained enough suitable targets to interest the newly arrived members of Fraser's team.

The main objective was to neutralise any remaining air strength that the enemy still possessed here so far to the rear of our main front; Task Force 111/2 was accordingly formed for the job under command of Rear-Admiral E. J. P. Brind, drawing on the British ships available at Manus.

This Task Force took departure at 1700 on the 12th June, organised as follows:

Task Unit 1:   The carrier *Implacable* with 21 Avengers, 11 Fireflies and 48 Seafires embarked.
Task Unit 2:   The escort carrier *Ruler*; cruiser *Swiftsure*; and destroyer *Termagant*.
Task Unit 5:   The cruisers *Uganda*, *Achilles* and *Newfoundland*.
Task Unit 15: The 24th Destroyer Flotilla: *Troubridge*, *Tenacious*, *Terpsichore* and *Teazer*.

Of these ships only the *Swiftsure* had had any extensive gunnery practice with the Pacific Fleet. The *Implacable's* most recent operation had been off the coast of Norway. The *Newfoundland* had taken part in the bombardment of Wewak in New Guinea on her way up to the forward area. It had originally been intended that the operation should comprise air strikes only, but soon after their departure they were informed that it was considered desirable to include surface bombardment as well, as it was envisaged that the cruisers would be so employed during the planned landings in Japan proper later in the year.

Admiral Brind therefore organised bombardment exercises for the ships while en-route for the target zone. The Task Force arrived in the aircraft launching area in the early evening of the 13th. It was planned to launch *Implacable's* strikes from a position some 85 miles 205 degrees east from Dublon Island at 0540 the following morning. In order to be in a covering position for the bombardment in good time, the surface striking force was detached so as to be within twenty miles of the area; this group—

Swiftsure, Newfoundland, Achilles, Uganda, Troubridge, Teazer and *Tenacious*—accordingly sped on ahead during the night.

By morning the carrier force was in position under lowering skies and heavy rain showers. The weather was clear over the islands and the initial sorties of strike and photo-reconnaissance aircraft were despatched as planned. The escort carrier *Ruler* had been included to provide an emergency flight deck and the wisdom of such a role was proven in the opening stages of the operation when some six Seafires landed aboard her; they had lost touch with *Implacable* due to the poor weather conditions which prevailed early on. In addition, with the big carrier busy ranging the aircraft of the second strike up on deck, any aircraft which got into trouble would have caused much confusion and delay had there not been an alternative deck available.

Luckily, as the day wore on, the flying conditions improved, and strikes were launched against the enemy stronghold at $2\frac{1}{2}$-hour intervals throughout the day. A CAP of eight fighters was constantly maintained over the carriers, and a similar number over the cruiser force. A United States submarine was also on hand to perform the useful Lifeguard rescue service for any of our pilots forced to ditch; American Catalina amphibious aircraft were also on hand, but in fact were not actually called upon.

The carrier continued to launch attacks all day from a position varying from sixty to eighty miles off from Dublon Island, but although our young airmen were eager to show their worth very few worthwhile targets were found in the islands. Enemy airborne reaction was meagre. A few of our returning planes were forced to ditch, but all aircrews were picked up by the *Terpsichore* and *Termagant*. At the conclusion of the strike programme the carriers withdrew and at dawn on the 15th made rendezvous once more with the cruisers. Admiral Brind aboard *Uganda* then organised his bombarding force into three units and proceeded to close Truk. The units comprised: *Newfoundland* and *Troubridge*; *Swiftsure* and *Teazer*; *Achilles*, *Uganda* and *Tenacious*, each group of cruisers having a destroyer attached for smoke-laying and counter-battery work if required.

The carrier force operated independently ten miles to the east, providing spotters and CAPs as required. Admiral Brind took his squadron in on an approach line designed to achieve surprise if possible and in this he was successful. Each cruiser had predetermined targets which should be engaged in case of communications failure during the run-in.

Swiftsure took the most northerly position and *Newfoundland* the southerly and engaged coastal defence batteries on Moen to the north and Uman Island to the south, while *Uganda* and *Achilles* in the centre took under fire the seaplane base at Dublon Island. All these ships opened fire simultaneously at 20,000 yards, firing thirty rounds per gun.

The shoot was less effective than had been hoped, due mainly to inexperience, but technical faults aboard *Uganda* contributed to this, as did the fact that only one spotter plane was provided to control the fire of both ships of the centre group. Ineffective fire was encountered by *Swiftsure* from her target, but this was silenced, *Newfoundland's* target was well hit and made no reply, she therefore shifted her fire to cover the Eten airstrip. Fire was ceased at 1110 when all ships withdrew to rejoin the carriers.

While this was going on *Implacable* continued to launch strikes which bombed and made rocket attacks on harbour installations, a floating dock, radio and radar stations and shore batteries. Only two enemy planes were destroyed, while flak damaged three of our aircraft. A novel feature insofar as the British Fleet was concerned was the launching of a night attack by six Avengers. The Americans had carriers especially fitted for night operations, which proved invaluable, but *Implacable's* small strike was the first occasion on which the Royal Navy had employed this system. In all the carrier flew some 113 offensive, and 103 defensive, sorties. If the targets were few and far between, the standards of flight launch and recovery attained during the operation were to stand them in good stead in the months ahead.

The force reassembled at dawn and set sail for Manus where they arrived on the 17th.

Here the fleet completed final storing before the sortie commenced. Manus was not a hospitable place for an enforced visit. The American base, was, of course, dry, although there was a bar ashore. Naturally the arrival of a British fleet was of considerable interest to the men of the US Navy ashore there and soon the various wardrooms of the fleet were chock-a-block with thirsty Americans, busily cementing Anglo-American relations over a glass.

It was while they were at Manus that Commander Lamb remembers an incident involving his own ship, which caused a few embarrassed moments. The *Implacable* had the reputation for having the finest bar in the fleet and on this particular night, on the eve of a big operation, everyone in the fleet seemed to be taking the opportunity for a last quick one before the day. The carrier was full of high-spirited Colonials at the time and it was therefore something of a bombshell when, in the midst of the revelry, a signal was received announcing the arrival of Admiral Vian for a surprise inspection. There was considerable panic in the air for, obviously, there was no time to clear up shipshape and tidy before he arrived. Just in time, some bright spark aboard came up with what can only be described as 'a brilliant innovation'.

When Admiral Vian stepped aboard he was met by a squad of the tallest matelots in the ship. The Admiral, immaculately attired in his white uniform, was thus adequately screened by these giants as he passed through the devastated areas and the visit passed off without untoward incident.

The Allied fleets were now preparing themselves to sail into the waters off Japan itself to take part in a huge softening up operation preparatory to a full scale invasion which was scheduled for some date in October, or not later than the 1st November. The Americans moved their Third Fleet to Leyte to replenish during June and by the 10th July this huge force, now back to full strength, was in position off Japan ready to start its pile-driver flattening of the main enemy strength. The first series of strikes against the Tokyo Plain caused widespread havoc and opposition proved surprisingly light. The American carrier-based planes ranged up and down the mainland leaving behind scores of burnt-out enemy aircraft littering the pock-marked runways of their home bases. Admiral McCain, the US carrier admiral, then moved north to Hokkaido and repeated the process, blitzing everything worthy of the name target.

Audaciously the Americans took their new battleships, supported by cruiser and destroyer squadrons, close inshore to pound and obliterate steel works and factories with their mighty 16-inch guns. Reaction from the enemy was still negligible and it was thought that he must be conserving his strength to throw against the main invasion force; the Allies did not yet realise how badly affected by fuel shortages the Imperial Navy and Army airforces and Naval Squadrons had become. On conclusion of this chilling display of power, Admiral Halsey took his ships back to the replenishment area to refuel. And here Admiral Rawlings and the rested BPF arrived to join him on 16th July, to play their part in the final defeat of Japan.

The carriers *Formidable*—Flag ship of Admiral Vian—and *Victorious* had sailed on the 28th June from Australian waters in company with the *King George V*, supported by some cruisers and destroyers; they arrived at Manus three days later where they were joined by Admiral Brind's squadron. Task Force 37, as it had now become to conform to American practice, then refuelled and sailed with the carriers *Formidable*, *Victorious*, and *Implacable*; *King George V*; the cruisers *Newfoundland*, *Achilles*, *Uganda*, *Euryalus*, *Gambia* and *Black Prince*; and the destroyers *Quiberon*, *Quickmatch*, *Quality*, *Quadrant*, *Troubridge*, *Tenacious*, *Termagant*, *Teazer*, *Terpsichore*, *Grenville*, *Undaunted*, *Undine*, *Urania*, *Urchin* and *Ulysses* to rendezvous with the Third Fleet. The battleship *Howe* had not completed her refit in South Africa and the carrier *Indefatigable* which joined them at Manus had to be left behind when she suffered a break-down of her air compressors. It was expected that she would join before too long, and she did in fact catch up on the 20th. *Uganda* sailed for refitting on July 27th being replaced by *Argonaut*.

Contact was made on the 16th and for the first time the men of Task Force 37 viewed with awe the mighty array of naval power which stretched away as far as the eye could see: sixteen aircraft carriers, ten modern battleships, two new battle-cruisers and endless cruisers and destroyer squadrons. Admiral Rawlings and Admiral Vian went aboard 'Mighty Mo', the battleship *Missouri*, flagship of Admiral Halsey, for discussion on the part to be played by Task Force 37.

The British had understood that the BPF was to operate in close company with the Third Fleet but would retain its independent command structure. Halsey, however, had orders to the effect that he was to take overall control of the force. In his frank way he offered Admiral Rawlings three alternatives. One, TF 37 could operate in close company with the Third Fleet and act as an additional Task Group within that fleet; it would not receive direct orders from Halsey himself, but would be privy to the orders he gave to the Third Fleet. Two, TF 37 could operate semi-independently some seventy miles from Halsey's force to maintain its separate identity. Three, TF 37 could be allocated 'soft-spots' in Japan to attack independently.

Admiral Rawlings had no hesitation at all in accepting the first proposal; Admiral Halsey recalls that 'my admiration for him began at that moment'.[1] At Pearl Harbour Admiral Nimitz had already told Halsey not to absorb the British Fleet into his force but as Admiral Vian records in his book *Action this Day*: 'Halsey, however, turned a blind eye, and from that moment we were for all intents and purposes part of his fleet.'

The BPF was now in a far better position than in May to fulfil the current objectives. To keep up with the Americans was to prove quite a task; fortunately the Fleet Train, though still inadequate, had been further reinforced and the testing period off Okinawa had ironed out many of their teething troubles. It took a great deal of very hard work from everyone, from Admiral Rawlings downwards, but there was great determination in the fleet to make it work and to prove that the Royal Navy could still provide a fleet to be proud of. They were to succeed. When Admiral Spruance expressed the opinion after 'Iceberg' that the British Fleet was now ready to work with the American, he was right; what defects remained were overcome by sheer will power, and also by the continued generosity of the Americans to meet our requests.

So in the afternoon of the 16th the combined fleets sailed towards the land of the rising sun to exact the final reckoning; the avenging of Pearl Harbour and Singapore was imminent.

[1] *Admiral Halsey's Story* (McGraw, Hill, 1947).

10

Wings over Tokyo

As the great concourse of ships silently took up their battle positions for the start of the offensive the stage was set for the final act of the mighty drama which had been played for over three years across the world's largest ocean. It would have been a sobering thing for the originators of the initial Japanese assault to have witnessed the assembling of the Allied fleets, rank on rank of powerful ships, the largest fleet in the history of the world, covering miles of sea, arrayed and awaiting dawn to unlease their tremendous destructive power against the Japanese homeland, a terrible revenge for that ill-starred attack on the 7th of December against Pearl Harbour.

The Allied navies had come a great distance along the hard road of war since the early days of continuing defeats. The success of this next offensive would be the culmination of the long series of bloody battles towards Japan from the high-tide mark of Japanese victory in 1942. Following the bitter clashes off Guadalcanal, the Allied navies had steadily, but without faltering, thrown back the Japanese from stronghold to stronghold, inflicting enormous casualties on them as they did so, until now they stood poised to deliver the final crushing blow to bring them to their knees. The proud all-conquering sailors of Nippon were about to receive their final and most bitter lesson in the art of war-making; something they had never dreamed of was now staring them in the face, abject defeat. And not just an isolated defeat in battle, but the complete and utter subjugation of the entire Japanese nation, a nation that until 1945 had never been defeated.

The final preliminaries had been completed with the fall of Okinawa, the last outpost guarding the mainland of Japan. The next blow must certainly fall on the homeland islands, a final knock-out blow to the heart of the nation.

It was true that Japan still had massive forces deployed on other fronts, Burma, Malaya, French Indo-China, numerous island garrisons and above all the huge standing army on the Chinese mainland. But these great armies were in fact hostages to Allied sea power. Japan was a collection of islands, the heart of the Nipponese empire was not surrounded by land, easily defended by her millions of fanatical soldiers, but by sea, open sea—and mastery of this open sea lay clearly and obviously in the hands of the Third Fleet.

All Japan's divisions, all her aircraft and stockpiles of munitions across the 'Co-Prosperity Sphere' were all as nothing; the way lay open to render these forces as useless and burdensome as the many smaller garrisons, starving and wasting away on lonely atolls where they had been marooned by the surging tide of the Allies' seaborne assaults. The million men in China were now as of little use to Japan as the handfuls of surviving soldiers hiding away in the depths of the New Guinea jungle.

The Allies, it is true, were still not all convinced that to defeat Japan one could concentrate on the home islands; they were still plugging persistently away in orthodox land campaigns on far-away fronts. MacArthur was clearing the Philippines; the Australians were in Borneo; the British were still banging way in Burma as they had for the last three years; but many prominent Japanese realised the vulnerability of the Island Empire and it was as plain to them as to the Allied Naval Commanders that what happened on those far away battlefields was largely irrelevant. What mattered was how long could the seaborne assault on Japan itself be delayed. With the approach of the vast Allied Armada it was obvious that their own 'Overlord' with its inevitable outcome was about to break over them, and behind the scenes a growing number of statesmen set about turning the nation's thoughts towards peace, albeit no longer a victorious one.

Everything on which the Empire depended was in her four home islands, her heavy industries, shipbuilding, armament works, great centres of population, agriculture. It was useless to suggest that, should Japan proper fall, the armies could carry on from the Chinese mainland. Had they attempted to do so their position would have been quite hopeless: no supplies of arms, ammunition or food would have reached them; they would have been surrounded, in a bitterly hostile land with no base, no front to identify themselves with and no objective other than survival.

The final battle must take place on the Tokyo Plain and nowhere else.

However, Japan's vast armies were not brought home in anticipation of this final battle; there was too deep a mistrust of Soviet Russia. The Japanese felt that Russia was merely biding her time, following the defeat of Germany and the rape of Eastern Europe, to move overwhelming forces eastwards and send them flooding across the Manchurian borders as soon as it suited her. This in fact was just what did happen, although Stalin's hand was to be forced in a way that no-one in Japan could foresee.

Before the fresh carrier-borne offensive opened, Japan was already a nation under siege. Her losses in merchant shipping through heavy and sustained mining of her coastal waters, very open to this type of blockade, had crippled her capacity to support herself for very much longer in raw materials from that part of her Empire still under her control. She was in fact virtually cut off from her overseas garrisons and supplies alike. To the toll of the minefields the United States Navy's submarine services added their tally, which ran into hundreds of thousands of tons destroyed. Even before the big American bombers carried out their massed raids on factories and industrial plants, total production was declining alarmingly as vital commodities went down in the ships of the mercantile service.

The waves and waves of Superfortress aircraft which were blackening the skies over Japan's major cities were another warning to the people of Nippon on how close their final reckoning lay. Each week brought another fearful total of cities burnt out and destroyed and enormous civilian casualties which further hit morale. Japan's own folly had left her without defences against any of these three assaults on her very existence. There had been no provision for escort vessels to defend her scattered merchant ships; no programme to combat heavy mining in the waters adjacent to her homeland; and no high-altitude fighter aircraft had been developed to combat the big four-engined bombers of the USAAF, which now approached their targets at their leisure and demolished cities with radar plotted accuracy—while Japanese airmen waited in their thousands for the signal to carry out their final devotions to their Emperor and throw themselves at the invasion fleet.

For, by June 1945, the Japanese Government had been reduced to this: the invasion was coming—that was clear—but, in order to smash it when it appeared, every fighter had to be husbanded in readiness for the fatal day. Thus the American air attacks continued almost unchecked in increasing scale and violence.

Japan could not avoid total defeat, but the enemy would pay dearly for every foot of Japanese soil. So stated the government which, despite the knowledge that by mid-summer of 1945 our nation was nearly prostrate, elected to conclude the war in a bath of blood by resisting the imminent invasion with every available man.[1]

It was widely expected on the Allied side that this in fact would be the case; with Okinawa very vividly in the forefront of their minds, they were convinced that any Allied landings on the Japanese home islands would be met by the usual fanatical resistance to which they were accustomed, but on a much wider scale. It was expected that casualties would be very high, but this would have to be borne in order to strike straight at the heart of Japan. The landings were scheduled for not later than November 1st—a date far in advance of any Japanese predictions. Again and again the unexpected surge of American strength across the Pacific had caught them on the hop; and the final move was to be no exception.

Although the indented, wooded coastline of Japan made defensive preparations easy, the speed of the Allied advance meant in effect that much of the defence network of the homeland was below standard; it was in no way as tough a nut to crack as Hitler's 'Atlantic Wall'—and even that had been breached on the first day. What was expected was fierce and vicious fighting once the troops were ashore, with unprecedented use of Kamikaze tactics in every form of warfare.

It was not known on the Allied side just how low the remaining oil stocks for the Imperial Navy were; all that could be ascertained was that, in numbers of ships anyway, the Japanese still had a formidable fleet; if this were to be used in conjunction with their total remaining air strength, the combination could pose a grave threat to any invasion convoy. To finally destroy the Japanese Navy and to test the strength of his airborne defences were now Admiral Halsey's two main objectives.

The Third Fleet was formed into four Task Forces at this time but, as one was refitting, the BPF took station in its place as the most northerly group of the fleet. There were two reasons for this: in this position the BPF, having the weakest defences, would not be

[1] *Zero* by Okumiya and Horikoshi: Cassell, 1957.

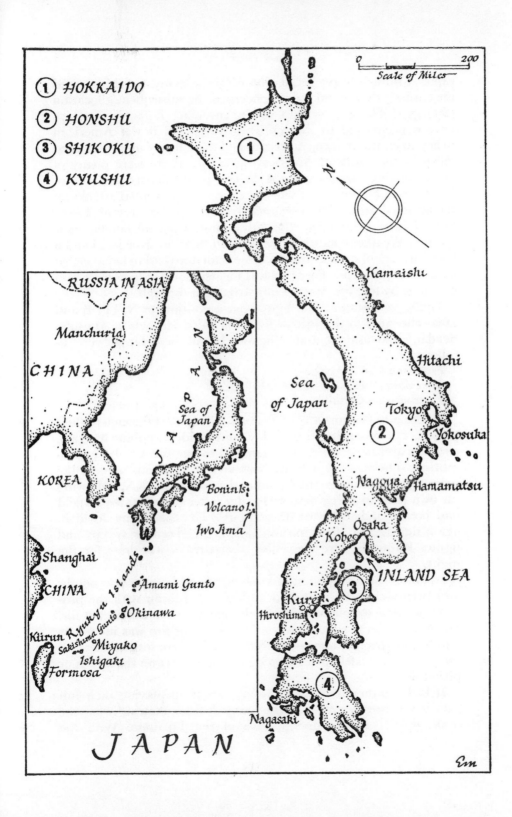

1 HOKKAIDO

2 HONSHU

3 SHIKOKU

4 KYUSHU

Scale of Miles

0   200

Kamaishi

Sea
of Japan

Hitachi

Tokyo

Yokosuka

Nagoya

Hamamatsu

Osaka

Kobe

INLAND SEA

Kure

Hiroshima

Nagasaki

RUSSIA IN ASIA

Manchuria

CHINA

Sea of
Japan

KOREA

Bonin Is.

Volcano I.

Iwo Jima

Shanghai

CHINA

Amami Gunto

Kiirun

Okinawa

Ryukyu Islands

Sakishima Gunto

Miyako

Ishigaki

Formosa

JAPAN

exposed to such heavy retaliation from the many airfields around the capital; the second point concerned the subsequent allocation of targets. The greater bulk of the surviving Japanese warships were concentrated to the south at Kure, and it was American policy to ensure that the destruction of these heavy units remained solely in the hands of American aircrews. There were plenty of other suitable targets and the British pilots showed no lack of initiative in finding them when the weather prevented attacks on the assigned areas. The vast industrial complexes around Tokyo formed ideal targets and the Navy pilots went all out on their mission. Weather conditions were found to be far from ideal and a large number of strikes from the American ships had to be cancelled because of this. Task Force 37 was luckier; some targets were also obscured by fog, but most of our strikes got through.

Flying off began at first light from a position 37°N, 143°E and areas allocated to the British flyers included airfields at Masuda, Sendai, Matrushima and Niigata. In all launchings were as follows:

Formidable—28 Corsairs.
Implacable—8 Fireflies and 12 Seafires.
Victorious—28 Corsairs.

Of these 16 Corsairs and 12 Seafires failed to get through to their targets. The others had a field day, and besides bombing hangars, runways and parked aircraft, managed to bag three railway locomotives. The strike which hit Niigata was an unofficial one, the strike leader, Lieutenant-Commander Baldwin, RN, following his own plan in flying across Honshu, after his allocated airfield had been found to be 'weathered out'. The conditions closed in again during the afternoon and all further bomber sweeps and fighter Ramrods were cancelled; the carriers withdrew for the night.

In all the BPF had planted some eighty-odd 500-pound bombs and twenty-eight 60-pound rockets across Honshu with the promise of more to follow. Nine of the enemy were accounted for, but none of these were airborne. Anti-aircraft fire was intense as had been expected, but only three Corsairs were lost; of these all the pilots were safely picked up by the destroyers on the screen or picket duty.

If bad weather prevented the carriers from playing their full part it was not to prevent *King George V* from showing what she could do to aid the discomfiture of the Japanese. With the escorting destroyers *Quality* and *Quiberon,* she parted company from Task Force 37 at 1430 and joined up with a bombarding squadron of American heavy ships. Their destination was the industrial area of Hatachi, about fifty miles north of Tokyo.

Her attack was carried out in extremely difficult weather conditions with rain and fog and poor visibility which made accurate navigation difficult and kept all the spotters grounded. Firing commenced at 2310 by radar control; *King George V* was allotted an unidentified factory area at which she pumped out 97 rounds of 14-inch HE. Her fire was then shifted to the Hatachi Engineering Division which was saturated with a further 91 heavy shells. The big ships continued their assault for an hour without opposition, the British battleship rounding off her night's performance with a 79 shell shoot at the Hatachi Engineering Tacha works: this site produced about a quarter of the total Japanese output of heavy electrical power plant and by the time the Allied squadron was finished the whole area was burning fiercely. Allied heavy and medium bombers had already given the area a good going over and the target was now considered written off. In addition to the tremendous destructive power of heavy naval gunfire, the fact that Allied battleships could carry out an uninterrupted shoot so close to Tokyo itself and escape unscathed was a heavy blow to enemy morale.

The three British ships took their departure at 0715 on the 18th and rejoined the carriers. By the time they rejoined the carrier force that afternoon the bombing programme was already well under way with heavy strikes directed against airfields around Tokyo. The weather had improved somewhat but the total of strikes sent out was reduced by the fact that salt water had leaked into the reserve petrol system of the *Victorious* which limited her to despatching only six Corsairs all day.

Implacable managed to get eight Fireflies and twenty Seafires up before conditions turned sour again and further sorties were cancelled. *Formidable* got away a Corsair Ramrod against Choshi and two hours later a further eight made attacks on Katari, destroying three float-planes moored in a nearby river. Again no airborne enemy was found, and our losses were light: two Corsairs both lost with their pilots, against twelve enemy destroyed and eighteen damaged. Two Seafires were also lost, their low endurance making it impossible for them to clear fog areas and forcing them to circle aimlessly until they had to ditch. The Americans meanwhile had made prolonged attacks with their main strength against the battleship *Nagato*—discovered intact at Yokosuka; they damaged her, but failed to sink her.

The weather was still poor on the 19th and there was a threat of a typhoon in the fuelling area. After some hanging about it was decided to withdraw and await more suitable conditions for maximum strikes to be mounted. The fleet steamed south to reach the replenishment zone early on the 20th.

Refuelling took place slowly; once again innumerable difficulties were encountered with hoses bursting under pressure and leakages. One oiler arrived some 2,500 tons short due to having replenished the *Indefatigable* which had made a high-speed dash up from Manus with the destroyers *Barfleur*, *Wrangler* and *Wakeful* to rejoin the fleet. The whole time-consuming process of oiling placed Admiral Rawlings in such difficulties that he was forced in the end to ask Admiral Halsey to fuel the 6-inch cruisers from American ships as otherwise he would not have been ready—and this in spite of a remission of 24-hours because of a postponement. To help make up our deficiency in oilers it was recommended to the Admiral Fleet Train that *Arbiter* and other escort carriers —she had actually refuelled the aircraft—should be converted to enable them to assist in the main oiling chore.

Replenishment was finally completed at 1900 on the 21st but the weather was still very bad and remained so until the 24th. During this period Admiral Halsey and his staff stayed aboard *King George V* with Admiral Rawlings for friendly discussions. Halsey had decided to shift his fleet's operational zone some four hundred miles to Shikoku to enable the Allies to hit hard at Japan's Inland Sea, thought to be rich in potential warship targets. Here anchored at Kure lay what remained of the once proud and invincible Imperial Battle Fleet. Now these massive ships lay immobilised through lack of fuel, awaiting their fate as huge floating anti-aircraft batteries.

The BPF however was given different and less alluring targets in the region around Osaka, where they might find warship targets 'of secondary importance'. Despite a feeling that the Americans had hogged the best hunting grounds for themselves, the men of Task Force 37 determined to make the best of it and when the weather finally cleared on the 24th they put up a maximum number of sorties, 416 from the four carriers.

In all fifteen offensive operations were mounted including five big combined strikes, a total of 227 British planes getting through to hit hard at all manner of shipping in the Inland Sea. Sixteen Corsairs from *Formidable* escorted twelve Avengers from *Implacable* to strike at Yokushima bomber airfield on Shikoku, these Avengers gaining the distinction—with twelve more from *Formidable's* 848 Squadron—of being the first British bombers to attack Japan proper. Despite heavy flak they inflicted severe damage to the field for the loss of one bomber.

Further bombing raids followed during the afternoon against Takamutsu airfield without loss. Meantime *Victorious's* bombers of 849 Squadron, led by Lieutenant-Commander A. J. Griffith, RNVR, combined with two Corsairs and two Fireflies to deliver a slashing attack on the Japanese aircraft carrier *Kaiyo*, leaving her on fire with her back broken. This type of target made up for the frustrating assaults on flak-lined airfields and they made the most of it. Shipping of every kind was strafed and bombed throughout the day, striking right across Honshu to the far coast in search of targets.

In addition to razing factories, dockyard installations and transport they bombed and sank the destroyer escorts *CD4* and *CD30*, damaged some others, destroyed 24 junks near Choshi, and attacked with rockets hangars north of Tokyo and railway facilities near Katori. Some thirteen enemy planes of all types were destroyed on the ground. Our losses totalled four aircraft in combat, as the enemy finally reacted to our disdainful use of his airspace. A few enemy planes made weak attempts to probe the fleet's defences, but were all easily intercepted and destroyed.

The Americans, too, were having an excellent day. Heavy and prolonged attacks were made with waves of bombers and rocket-firing fighters from the Third Fleet which crushed even the strong anti-aircraft defences around Kure Naval Yard. The battleships *Ise*, *Hyuga* and *Haruna*, the carrier *Amagi*, five cruisers and several destroyers made up the impressive bag scored by the Americans in three days' work. The proud Japanese Navy had virtually ceased to exist.

The 25th repeated the successful pattern of the 24th for Task Force 37. The weather was very bad early on over targets and only one Avenger released its bomb-load—on an unidentified factory—but later strikes reached installations and airfields on Shikoku, strafing flak batteries, aircraft, and a seaplane base. Twelve enemy aircraft were destroyed on the ground, two freighters, a large cargo ship and several junks were attacked and left aflame on the Inland Sea.

The continued successes against what were obviously major targets caused a general uplift in the morale of the fleet at this time—and for the aircrews there was also the knowledge that, if they were shot down and captured alive by the Japanese, they would not be beheaded. Captain Halliday, who came very near to a forced-landing at Palembang, records:

> Strange as it may seem, conditions for captured aircrew were far more civilized over Japan than over Sumatra. At this stage of the war, capture meant a turn in a Japanese prisoner of war camp and, while this was not a very happy experience, it made a sharp contrast to what they could expect over Sumatra or Java where they could not help knowing that, if they were shot down and taken alive, they were in for a pretty grisly end.

Another big morale-booster at this time was the fact that aircrew were now being relieved much earlier than had been usual throughout the war until now. A feeling of resentment had built up against the Fleet Air Arm in general that pilots were expected to keep going until they were either killed or mentally exhausted.

> One saw an enormous number of one's friends killed, or go missing, or just not come back [a former pilot remembers]. One literally had a carrier full of replacement crews following the fleet around and every time the ship replenished this carrier would ferry fresh crews aboard and take off the wounded. One got the feeling that life was a very short term proposition.

The pilots were not too interested in the grand strategy, in the whys and wherefores of the thing—they were too busy keeping up with their work. This was something that Admiral Vian had tackled early, and by 1945 his efforts were bearing fruit. Commander Hay, then Air Co-ordinator on *Victorious*, thought that Vian personally made a great contribution to the success of the British Task Force and won the gratitude and respect of all the aircrews.

> We were all a little apprehensive when we learned of his appointment as Carrier Admiral to the BPF and had visions of the Fast Carrier Squadron steaming at full speed, like a destroyer flotilla, into the nearest Japanese harbour with Vian shouting 'The Navy's

here!' But he turned out to be a very different type of person to what we had expected, quite a shy man in fact—but very efficient.

He at once confessed that his knowledge of carrier operations was very limited and he expressed a willingness to learn from us. He quickly became an excellent Carrier Admiral and, like a select few admirals, including especially Admiral Sir James Somerville, he was very quick to grasp the essentials of Air/Sea warfare.

We all felt very fortunate in his selection. He quickly earned the thanks of the BPF aircrews by the interest which he showed in their well-being and he always kept his word. When we first arrived in the Pacific the standard period of front-line combat duty for the US Navy aircrews was six months and Vian promised us that everyone in the BPF would be rested after the same period of time. This promise he made work. I cannot describe the tremendous boost in morale it caused among the pilots and navigators of the carriers. They had expected to grind away month after month supporting the American offensives ashore without any hope of relief, such had been the impression of carrier operations which they had picked up in training establishments ashore.

Much elated after such a rewarding period the fleet withdrew that evening to refuel, but not before the enemy made further belated attempts to hit back at them. With the masses of aircraft returning to the fleet, it was surprising that the enemy had not tried to intermingle before; on this occasion, certainly, it almost paid off.

Several high flying reconnaissance aircraft had been plotted over the fleet during this period but it was not until dusk on the 28th when the last strikes were flying on to their carriers that the enemy made a move. Evidently relying on avoiding identification amid the many groups of returning Allied planes, some thirty or so Grace bombers in small groups attempted to carry out surprise torpedo attacks. They were initially successful in their penetration of the radar plots but fortunately Commander E. D. Lewin of the Air Direction team felt uneasy about one such incoming group and alerted the only British aircraft still airborne.

These were four Corsairs and two Hellcats from *Formidable*, the former just about at the end of their fuel endurance and not equipped for night fighting. They were vectored out to intercept the suspicious contact, and, on first sighting, at once identified them as hostile. The two Hellcats, piloted by Lieutenant Atkinson and Sub-Lieutenant McKie, at once dived straight into the enemy formation and quickly shot down three of the bombers as the fourth fled the scene. Other hostile groups were immediately identified and night fighters were scrambled from the specially adapted night-fighting carrier with the US Task Force, the *Bonhomme Richard*. They dealt very effectively with two other enemy formations and no hostile aircraft got through to the fleet. All the same, it had been a close thing, emphasising the fact that any slight relaxation in vigilance could very easily cost the Allies valuable ships; a dusk torpedo bomber attack is very difficult to detect and, at close range, there is little time for successful avoiding action.

It was during this skirmish that one aircraft of *Formidable's* CAP, out of fuel, made contact with an American carrier and received permission to make an emergency landing aboard her. The American deck-landing procedure was entirely different to our own and there followed a frantic few moments as the British pilot attempted to touch down—using what he knew of the American technique—while the despairing American batman was trying to guide him safely on deck with British signals. Happily the pilot succeeded at the second attempt, although the landing was subsequently described as 'very ropy indeed'.

The fleet then withdrew on the evening of the 25th to replenish. The dramatic switching of targets from one end of Japan to the other with just a few hours' notice was a classic illustration of the advantages of sea power. The four great Task Forces could strike hard at a target one day, only to reappear two days' later in a totally different area. It was impossible for the Japanese to anticipate the next zone to be struck and their morale suffered accordingly. For the BPF with its shoe-string logistics' system, the pace set by Halsey, coupled with their other problems, was a hot one. Admiral Rawlings reported that his fleet sometimes had the greatest difficulty in keeping up. On one occasion, as recalled by Admiral Vian, the entire assembly of the Third Fleet was withdrawing out to sea while Task Force 37 was steaming straight into the Bay of Tokyo in order to recover some of *Implacable's* Seafires!

Despite this the BPF maintained a record number of sorties throughout this dramatic period and the Americans were full of praise for the way the British maintained their offensive capability despite their many handicaps. The British, being on the outside wing of the three American groups, had no direct contact with the C-in-C who led the whole Force from the centre American group and had thus to rely on all his major signals being relayed via the nearest group, which could cause some delay; a further difficulty arose because the British fleet's maximum speed was restricted to the twenty-eight knots of the *King George V*—and the big carriers could only do 30 knots, anyway—whereas the American battle-ships, carriers, cruisers, and destroyers were all capable of attaining thirty-two knots. It was planned that when enough of the new light fleet carriers arrived on station—four were on their way—a second British Task Force would be formed around them and the battleships *Duke of York* and *Anson*, also recently arrived. This would have posed even greater problems as these smaller carriers were two or three knots slower even than the battleships. In the event the planning for a second British Force was overtaken by events and it never materialized.

Fuelling took place during the 26–27th some 700 miles away from the original planned position, which added to Admiral Fisher's problems in keeping up supplies. Two of the four tankers which formed the oiling force had never taken part in actual afloat refuelling before. One, which had been converted for the purpose in a last minute rush before being despatched, could only carry out refuelling in the abeam position; a second could only fuel from one side and, even after a quick refit at Manus after arriving there from Colombo with numerous defects, she had a top speed of only $7\frac{1}{2}$ knots! Fuelling from these four ships was so slow that once again Admiral Halsey had to replenish *Newfoundland* and *Achilles* from American oilers.

The Task Forces were back in position early on the 28th and resumed strikes at targets around the Inland Sea. The BPF flew off some 155 aircraft of which 118 made attacks. One Avenger was lost. Again they ranged far and wide over Honshu and Shikoku adding to their already impressive tally of shot-up planes, burnt-out hangars and coastwise shipping. Towards afternoon the weather once more took a hand and severely curtailed later flying operations. Despite this it was a successful day for flying operations and saw the Americans complete the destruction of Japan's re-maining naval units.

King George V repeated her earlier bombarding performance; with the destroyers *Undine*, *Ulysses* and *Urania*, she was detached to form Task Group 37/12 and joined an American bombardment force under Rear-Admiral Badger.

Her particular target was the 'Japanese Musical Instrument Works' near Tokyo, a large complex now devoted to the manufacture of aircraft propellers. The weather was foggy as the big ships neared the coast and on the final approach the *Urania* and *Ulysses* were involved in a minor collision, but managed to remain with the group.

The British battleship opened fire at 2319 at 20,075 yards range and made individual practice in clear moonlight with spotters from the American fleet operating for her. In twenty-seven minutes she despatched some 265 rounds of 14-inch HE into the factory area. There was no reply from ashore to this massive deluge of shells, although the *Undine* fired frequently on small craft seen inshore; it was thought that these might be suicide boats, of which the enemy was known to have huge numbers in readiness for the expected invasion. It was later learnt that through an error on the part of the spotting aircraft a large number of shells fell outside the factory area, but those that did land on target were sufficient to halt production, the workers refusing to go back and face such a bombardment again.

King George V and her escorts rejoined the next day and the fleet moved to a new position. This time the targets for our bombers included Nagoya Bay and Maizuri and other areas in southern Honshu. The BPF put up 216 planes of which some 192 made attacks. The Harima shipyard was heavily hit, the Avengers claiming a 5,000-ton freighter amongst their victims. Other targets hit hard and often included Ise Wan. Two planes of 1842 Squadron were hit and forced to ditch, 'almost inside a Jap harbour', but the crews were picked up safely by one of the ubiquitous American Lifeguard submarines.

Airborne opposition was now growing far heavier and eight British planes were lost, though far heavier casualties were taken from the enemy. At Maizuri three Japanese destroyers were found and given a thorough going over, leaving two of them on fire from stem to stern and one, the *Okinawa*, sinking. Admiral Rawlings then withdrew early hoping to get a flying start on his Allies and complete his replenishment in time to commence the next two-day strike period.

There was no real feeling in July 1945 that we were about to make a final effort [Admiral Denny recalls]; we were all so attuned to war conditions by then that really it did not seem to matter whether the war would finish within three weeks or ten. But if, for example, we thought we would have to fly another twenty days of strikes and a pilot was obviously reaching the limit of his endurance, he would be forbidden to fly; no one was ever allowed to go beyond the limit. We did get to the stage where we knew that certain pilots were approaching this limit and they had to be cut out of flying duties at once. This had the effect, over a period, in the four or five carriers combined, of eating into our strength, although, fortunately, we were well supplied with replacement air crew of a high standard.

It was only this gradually increasing erosion of air crew which Admiral Denny considered as an important factor in the assessment of how much longer Task Force 57 could maintain the pressure. It seems clear that the fleet was already so fully extended that the possibility of a hotting-up of operations against Japan could not be seriously considered.

Total claims for this period just completed amounted to one destroyer, two oilers, nine small freighters and seventeen junks sunk; two destroyers, two submarines, seven coasters, one oiler and a hundred small craft were damaged, as well as a score of enemy aircraft.

Only one day had been allowed for refuelling and it was thought exceedingly doubtful if TF 37 could meet this deadline, but fate intervened in the shape of several typhoons in their immediate vicinity, which ensured that no operations could be carried out for almost a week. The severe storms on the fringes of the typhoon areas kicked up a heavy swell which made replenishing an even more difficult task than usual, especially for the destroyers. The sorry list of burst hoses continued; on top of this one oiler arrived some 750 tons short due to a hasty refuelling turn-around. Admiral Fisher was having his meagre resources stretched to the utmost to keep the Fleet on station.

Fuelling commenced at 1000 on the 31st—again two of the oilers were new to the job—and proceeded at a slow pace throughout the day. The *King George V* managed to carry out a slow embarkation of 14-inch ammunition from the *Robert Maersk*, but when *Victorious* attempted to bomb up from the same ship she found that the rising swell made the handling of the 500-pound bombs quite impossible, their supplier being such a tiny ship in relation to the big carrier. The attempt had to be abandoned.

Attempts to carry on with replenishment continued throughout the next two days without much progress being made and it was not until the 2nd August that the weather moderated sufficiently to allow the job to be successfully completed. With the imminent threat of a hurricane the combined fleet then moved to a safer area.

The strikes scheduled for the 3rd—against targets in the vicinity of Hiroshima—were abruptly cancelled and the fleet was ordered to sail clear of the area. Speculation on the reasons for this was silenced when the news was released that the first Atomic Bomb had been dropped and had obliterated the city of Hiroshima. The world was on the brink of a new and terrible age of fear and horror. The leaders had decided that the use of this weapon was justified if it would bring forward surrender; certainly the estimates of Allied casualties for the forthcoming invasion, Operation 'Olympic', were staggering, and the operation was bound to be protracted.

Before sailing northwards it had been estimated that the fleet would need to refuel again on the 4th and this was known to be beyond the capabilities of our Logistic Support.

In the meantime the cruisers *Gambia* and *Newfoundland*, and the destroyers *Terpsichore*, *Termagant* and *Tenacious*, had joined a US bombardment force which sailed to complete the destruction of the Japanese Ironworks at Kamashi. With the *South Dakota* and *Indianapolis* providing spotters, the British cruisers opened fire at 1245 for a two-hour period. The target was pulverised and several enemy aircraft which tried to get through to the force were shot down by the CAP provided from the fleet.

A further bombardment was planned using *King George V*, three 6-inch cruisers and escorting destroyers to take place on the 13th, although due to the fuel situation it was expected that several of these would only be able to get back to Manus under tow, but the plans were cancelled because of the atomic attacks, and also because of a long-standing machinery defect affecting two shafts of the battleship.

On the 9th Admiral Rawlings continued striking at the enemy from a position off the north-east of Honshu, where a large number of untouched enemy airfields were located. Mass attacks from the combined fleets inflicted very heavy losses on the enemy. Some 250 planes were destroyed on the ground, TF 37 claiming fifty of them; in all the British made 236 launchings for offensive sorties of which 227 reached their targets. Special attention was paid to the shipping at Onegawa harbour. Two auxiliaries were sunk, the *Kongo Maru 2* and the *Takuanan Maru 6*, and many small ships shot up, but most pilots concentrated on the destroyers and escort vessels lying there.

It was here that a gallant attack by Lieutenant R. H. Gray, RCNVR, won him a posthumous Victoria Cross, the final one awarded in the war. Leading his section of Corsairs in a very low-level bomb and rocket attack on an enemy destroyer through thick flak, his plane was caught in a cross-fire from several enemy vessels and badly hit. Regardless of this he continued his approach, scoring a direct hit which sank his target before crashing into the harbour.

Other planes from *Formidable* shot up airfields, harbour areas and damaged shipping at Shiogama, while Avengers from the same ship hit Matsushima airbase with good effect.

The attacks continued without pause on the 10th. Once again Onegawa was the target, but by this time Allied planes had sunk everything in sight and British strikes moved on to Sendai and the coastal plain. Limited visibility between the launching position and the target areas made navigation difficult, but nevertheless airfields were struck and an escort vessel sunk. Airfields at Matsushima, Matsuda and Koriyama were worked over to eliminate any aircraft remaining, the total bag amounting to some eight destroyed and seven damaged. Lack of shipping and aircraft targets diverted many strikes to rail termini, locomotives and tracks and a large amount of rolling stock was written off.

This two-day effort by the combined fleets accounted for some 700 enemy aircraft and broke the back of the air defences in northern Honshu. The Japanese, who up to now had been husbanding their strength, seemed to realise that their power was ebbing away and they were stung into response. Heavy Kamikaze and orthodox raids were sent against the Allied fleet throughout this period. Very few survived and the fighter CAPs had a field day. Frustrated, many of the enemy vented their spite on four American pickets to the south. Ignoring heavy losses they concentrated on these unfortunate ships and succeeded in hitting, and severely damaging, the *Borie*. This was their sole success.

On the 9th August, the second Atomic Bomb was dropped and annihilated Nagasaki. The Russians, sensing easy pickings, swept across their frontiers into Manchuria. There was now no hope for the Japanese and many at long last realised it. On the 10th, the Japanese negotiators agreed to most of the Allied terms, but still held out for the Emperor to be left on the throne. While this point was being thrashed out, the killing went on.

In order to keep up a heavy pressure on the wavering enemy Admiral Halsey decided to mount further assaults. Fuelling took place on the 11th and, at a conference held aboard the *Missouri*, Admiral Rawlings agreed to co-operate to the best of his ability. It proved impossible to retain the whole of Task Force 37 on station, our support facilities just could not run to it, but Rawlings agreed to maintain a token force with TF 38 until Admiral Fraser arrived with reinforcements. The Commander-in-Chief was at this time aboard *Duke of York* at Guam, but on hearing of the imminence of the Japanese surrender he at once hurried north.

It was sad that the bulk of the Task Force which had fought so well against the enemy would not be in at the kill, but our previous plans had called for our withdrawal to Australia on the 10th in order to be at full strength for the actual launching of 'Olympic'; Halsey's targets were far to the north of Japan and our Fleet Train would be completely inadequate for such a major extension.

Admiral Rawlings therefore formed Task Group 38/5 to operate as the most northerly Task Force of the Third Fleet for these final operations. This group comprised *King George V*, *Indefatigable*, the cruisers *Gambia* and *Newfoundland*, and the destroyers *Barfleur*, *Napier*, *Nizam*, *Wakeful*, *Wrangler*, *Troubridge*, *Termagant*, *Tenacious* and *Teazer*. These vessels were fully topped up on the 11th, *King George V* being invited to fuel from the American oiler *Sabine* while *Missouri* fuelled from the other side—an impressive sight—while the rest of the fleet sailed for Manus.

Bad weather once more prevented the planned operations on the 12th but next day the fleet was in position and launched attacks against targets in the Tokyo plain. *Indefatigable's* first strike was airborne at 0400 from a position 34N, 142E to hit the Tokyo area, but on arrival in the target area found conditions too murky to identify their positions. They bombed some camouflaged factories instead.

The Japanese continued to try to break through the fleet's defences with large numbers of bomber and suicide sorties but the CAPs were on their toes and no enemy penetrated to with twenty-five miles of the ships. Some 250 enemy planes were destroyed on the ground and 150 damaged, while 21 were lost attacking the fleet. That evening the task force withdrew, refuelled next day, and were back in position on the 15th.

Indefatigable's first strike was again off at first light and this time they were jumped over the target by a force of twelve Zero fighters. A vicious dog-fight developed during which eight of the enemy were shot down for the loss of one Seafire. The Avengers bombed their sector and returned without loss except for one which was forced to ditch near the fleet. This marked the final offensive sortie of the BPF. At 0700 Admiral Nimitz cancelled all further offensive operations due to the acceptance of all Allied terms by the Japanese.

Some of the enemy just could not take this defeat and during the morning several Kamikazes approached the Task Force in last ditch attempts at final immortality. At 1120 a Judy was detected over the British group and at once commenced a dive on *Indefatigable* dropping two bombs which were very near misses. He was taken under fire and a few moments later was splashed by the CAP which had wisely been left in operation over the fleet. Several others were shot down during the day in spasmodic attacks which followed the signal from C-in-C:

> All enemy aircraft approaching the fleet are now to be shot down in a friendly manner.

These isolated sorties were the enemy's last fling; for the men of the Combined Allied Fleets it marked the vindication of four years of bloody struggle. All that now remained was the mopping up.

11

Retrospect

Although in theory the Japanese had finally accepted the surrender terms, they had not done so in fact and there still remained a huge army in combat readiness ashore supported by several thousand aircraft, dispersed but operational. In addition, spread over the huge tracts of occupied territory were many thousands of fighting men with able and fanatical commanders. How would they react?—would they accept the surrender or would they follow Admiral Ugaaki and prefer to go down in a gory act of self-destruction rather than admit defeat.

No one could be sure, so that the men of Task Force 37 sailed to accept the surrender of the enemy fully prepared for a fight. Admiral Fraser had already received instructions regarding the reoccupation of Hong Kong despite some interchanges between General Chiang Kai-shek and the Americans who refused to associate themselves in any way with the retaking of former 'Colonial territory'. The 'holier than thou' attitude adhered to at this time by the United States went very deep and certainly did not help to restore stability in the areas freed from Japanese conquest. General MacArthur is on record as saying that the failure of the Allies to liberate Java was one of the 'grave mistakes of the war', the subsequent civil war which followed bearing him out.

Nevertheless the newly arrived 11th Aircraft Carrier Squadron, *Glory*, *Colossus*, *Venerable* and *Vengeance*; the 2nd Battle Squadron, *Anson* and *Duke of York*; several cruisers and destroyers; together with the refitted *Indomitable* and the ships of TF 38/5 were together a formidable enough force to break any armed opposition and they were formed into Task Groups to effect the re-occupation of our former Empire.

For Hong Kong, Admiral Harcourt was put in command of a

force comprising *Indomitable, Venerable,* the cruisers *Swiftsure* and *Black Prince,* and the destroyers *Kempenfelt, Ursa, Quadrant* and *Whirlwind.* Another squadron under the command of Rear-Admiral Daniel and consisting of the *Anson* and *Vengeance* was earmarked to accept the surrender of Singapore, but due to further logistics problems was added to the Hong Kong force. The surrender of Singapore was left instead to the East Indies Command; Admiral Walker received the Japanese local commanders aboard the *Nelson* off Penang on the 2nd September, while Admiral Power entered the Singapore base itself the next day aboard the cruiser *Cleopatra.* The final surrender terms were ratified at Singapore by Admiral Mountbatten on the 12th.

To reoccupy Shanghai the BPF despatched the *Colossus,* the cruisers *Bermuda* and *Argonaut,* and the destroyers *Tyrian, Tumult, Tuscan* and *Quiberon,* under the command of Rear-Admiral Servaes. The *Glory* and the frigates *Hart* and *Amethyst* were despatched to Rabaul, while the heavy cruiser *Cumberland* went to Batavia with two frigates.

In the meantime Admiral Fraser had joined the BPF aboard the *Duke of York* on the 19th August, and on that day Admiral Halsey came aboard to make a broadcast to the British Commonwealth. The units of Task Group 38/5 anchored in Tokyo Bay and on the 2nd September the formal and final surrender took place aboard the USS *Missouri.*

At nine o'clock Admiral Nimitz and General MacArthur watched as General Umezu of the Japanese Imperial General Staff signed the historic documents, Admiral Fraser signing on behalf of Great Britain. At the end of the twenty minute ceremony some 450 aircraft from the Combined Fleets roared overhead. This symbolic display of sea/air power, the primary means of both Japan's early victory and of her present defeat, was a fitting one.

But over all the celebrations there lay the long shadow of the Atomic Bomb. Sea power at the supreme moment of its vindication was faced with the greatest ever threat to its future as the prime instrument of defence.

There was little thought of this, however, during the months of August and September. Celebration was the keynote; the most world-embracing war of all time was finally over. In the Victory Parade held in Sydney on 31st August the crews of the *Implacable, Formidable, Victorious, Black Prince, Grenville* and *Urania* all took part.

Then came another consideration, the repatriation of thousands of Allied and Commonwealth prisoners of war after years of hellish captivity. The great men-of-war which had so recently been steaming against a deadly foe now were turned into 'Mercy Ships' to bring back these emaciated men, their less fortunate comrades in arms. Fleet carriers, their aircraft dumped ashore, were converted into Hospital and Transport ships, embarking medical teams and supplies to carry out their new missions. Thus it was that the BPF carried out its final tasks throughout the months of October and November. Gradually the fleet in eastern waters was run down, as ship after ship departed for home, flying their long paying-off pendants. By the New Year the British fleet had been reduced to one cruiser squadron and a destroyer flotilla. The navy did not seem necessary any more.

The reasons are not hard to find. The postwar image of sea power was a distorted one. The picture of the *Prince of Wales* sinking under air attack was a public one; the scene of the *King George V* bombarding the Japanese mainland within a few miles of Tokyo some four years later was the forgotten side of the coin.

The use of the Atomic Bomb to bring about Japan's surrender established an awesome precedent. Certainly, as was the intention, it saved the lives of countless Allied fighting men; this is its justification. But, it may be asked, would not Japan have surrendered anyway, without an invasion. There is no simple answer to this question, but there is some disturbing evidence which supports the theory that she would indeed have been forced to surrender *before* the Allies invaded, despite the attitudes of her more militant leaders, and despite her huge standing army.

Naturally the bomb, so colossal in scale, so destructive and so new, held the world's attention, dominated all thinking related to the war and left little room for speculation at the time other than that the bomb alone had brought about the rapid surrender. Post-war examination of the state that Japan found herself to be in, prior to Hiroshima, have since caused some misgivings.

It can be said without fear of contradiction that in July 1945 Japan was utterly beaten, but that she would not face the fact. Her economy was in ruins, and this was brought about well before the Atomic Bomb was dropped. Industrial production was at a catastrophic low. This was the situation compared with the highest output figures of the war: iron production was down by

65 per cent; coal production by 29 per cent; chemicals by 48 per cent; and liquid fuels by 66 per cent. In some of the major factory complexes 96 per cent of the plant had been destroyed. In food supplies the situation was just as critical; by July 1945 the staple food ration per adult person was reduced by ten per cent to 312 grammes of staple food. Meat was reduced by 20 per cent, fish by 30 per cent and it was admitted that famine was possible, all outside food supplies having by this time been completely cut off.

Rail and road communications across the main islands by daylight was virtually impossible, the Allied air sweeps shooting up anything that moved. The great drain made by the armed services on manpower had reduced dockyard labour to negligible proportions, but this mattered little as by this time Japan, a nation of islands and inter-connecting sea transport by ferries and coastwise shipping, had had all its water-borne transport annihilated. Those few vessels surviving huddled in concealed creeks and rivers afraid to venture out into Japan's seas where they would be met with continual air and submarine assault and the dangers of thickly sown minefields.

Heavy bomber raids had reduced all the major cities to ashes. These raids and warship bombardments had caused hideous casualties—200,700 dead and 273,000 injured—and these figures do *not* include the Atomic Bomb casualties. Chaos and corruption was widespread and it was generally believed that the war could not possibly be won and that further fighting was senseless and indeed hopeless.

Looming large over this confusion was the threat of the Soviet Union. Japan had refrained from declaring war on Russia in 1941, even though this had enabled Stalin to transfer his Siberian divisions to Central Europe to grind down Japan's Axis partners. There was considerable hope that Russia would therefore refrain from attacking Japan in the rear. That this hope was a slender one was obvious to anyone who examined their treatment of Poland and other nations with whom they had no quarrel, and indeed it was this fear that led to the continued stationing of a vast army in China.

There can be little doubt that Stalin would have gone to war with Japan once his troop build-up had been completed; the dropping of the Bomb merely forced his hand in exactly the same way that Germany's rapid defeat of France in 1940 had led Mussolini to scramble to gain a share in the spoils.

It can reasonably be assumed that, faced with massive Soviet military activity on her flanks, with her industry and cities in ruins, her transport paralysed, even the most militant of Nipponese leaders could not have long delayed negotiations towards total surrender. Indeed, several peace feelers had already been put out.

The Bomb certainly did more in the shaping of future defence policy than any other weapon before or since. All the old lessons, abandoned in the twenties and thirties, and only relearnt at terrible cost, were again cast aside as obsolete. In a welter of new theories everything appertaining to sea power was relegated, in Britain anyway, to a limbo of meaningless phrases.

Since 1945 we have seen a long period of argument and decline. Despite overwhelming evidence as to the absolutely critical dependence of island nations, like Japan and Great Britain, on Sea Power, the Royal Navy has been reduced steadily, year by year. Excuses vary: 'retrenchment following the end of the war' was the first. Others followed: 'the Atomic Bomb'; 'reliance on NATO eliminates the need for Britain to go it alone at sea'; 'the use of air power to control the seas'—no-one calculated how many airliners would be needed to keep these islands supplied by air; and now we have 'the economy of the nation'.

As the ships dwindled, the reassurances grew more and more feeble, both in their content and their persuasion. 'We are still the greatest Sea Power after America' was replaced by 1957 by 'We are the third largest Sea Power' and now we are down to 'the largest naval contributor to NATO'.

All the time the number of active ships in the fleet grows fewer and fewer. In the late fifties we abandoned the Mediterranean 'in order to concentrate in the Far East'. In the mid-sixties we abandoned the Far East 'in order to concentrate in Home Waters'. By 1968 the Editor of *Jane's Fighting Ships* was having to report to an uninterested nation that the Royal Navy is now so reduced as to be hardly adequate to fulfil its peacetime commitments and completely inadequate to fight a war.

By contrast the Soviet Union is building up the largest fleet in its history, with no other reason for its existence than ocean warfare against the Atlantic lifeline and infiltration throughout the Mediterranean and Indian Ocean. Soviet sailors throng the streets of Alexandria where the last British sailors were thrown out as occupiers and aggressors. The recent plan to scrap our few remaining aircraft carriers is followed by announcements that the Soviets are building them for the first time.

Leader after leader has stepped forward with pleas to rebuild the Royal Navy; from Winston Churchill to General Montgomery, they have stated that the sea is our basic defence and also our greatest weakness. These appeals have fallen on deaf ears.

Now, even the RAF is growing concerned at the strength and growth of Russian naval might, but our fleet continues to dwindle in manpower and especially in the number of active ships.

On the 1st March, 1942, when our maritime condition was at its nadir, a scholar and sailor of outstanding ability in his generation, who had spent his life in studying and teaching the purpose and meaning of sea power to Britain, wrote these words of doubt, even agony of mind, on the typescript of an unpublished book: 'Now everything is in the melting pot, and whether after this war there will again be a Navy, or whether the country will interest itself and take steps to ensure that its people are made aware of the importance of sea power, and taught, not only by our terrible experience of tampering with the Navy in those fateful years since 1918, but also by the long experience of the past, I cannot tell. I greatly fear that what has happened before will repeat itself . . .' He then echoed Edmund Burke's earlier warning that 'of all the public services, the Navy is the one in which tampering may be of the greatest danger, which can be worst supplied in an emergency, and of which failure draws after it the largest and heaviest train of consequences'.[1]

[1] Note by Sir Herbert Richmond, Master of Downing College, Cambridge, written on the typescript of *The Navy as an Instrument of Policy* and quoted by Captain S. W. Roskill, the Official Historian in *The War at Sea*, Vol. III, H.M.S.O., 1961.

APPENDIX 1

COMPOSITION OF THE BPF MAY 1945

(Abbreviated list—for further particulars, decorations, etc., see Appendix 2)

BATTLESHIPS
King George V	Captain T. E. Halsey.
Howe	Captain H. W. U. McCall.

FLEET CARRIERS
Indomitable	Captain J. A. S. Eccles.
Victorious	Captain M. M. Denny.
Illustrious	Captain C. E. Lambe.
Indefatigable	Captain Q. D. Graham.

LIGHT CRUISERS
Swiftsure	Captain P. V. MacLaughlin.
Gambia	Captain R. A. B. Edwards.
Black Prince	Captain G. V. Gladstone.
Argonaut	Captain W. P. McCathy.
Euryalus	Captain R. Oliver-Bellasis.

DESTROYERS
Grenville	Captain H. P. Henderson.
Ulster	Lt-Cdr. R. J. Harrison.
Undine	Cdr. T. C. Robinson.
Urania	Lt.-Cdr. D. H. P. Gardiner.
Undaunted	Lt.-Cdr. T. C. E. R. Sharp.
Quickmatch	Cdr. O. Becker.
Quiberon	Lt.-Cdr. G. F. E. Knox.
Quality	Lt.-Cdr. The Viscount Jocelyn.
Queenborough	Cdr. P. L. Saumarez.
Kempenfelt	Captain E. G. MacGregor.
Whirlwind	Cdr. W. A. F. Hawkins.
Wessex	Lt.-Cdr. R. Horncastle.
Whelp	Cdr. G. A. F. Norfolk.
Wager	Lt.-Cdr. R. C. Watkin.

THE FLEET TRAIN MAY 1945

Rear Admiral Fisher aboard *Tyne*.

Escort Carriers (Replenishment):
Striker, Speaker, Ruler, Slinger.

Escort Carriers (Ferry Duties):
Fencer, Chaser.

Destroyers:
Napier, Nizam, Nepal, Norman.

Escort Vessels:
Crane, Pheasant, Woodcock, Whimbrel, Avon, Findhorn, Parret.

Landing Ship:
Lothian.

L.S.I.:
Empire Spearhead, Glenarm, Lamont.

Repair Ships:
Artifex, Resource.

Light Fleet Carrier (Repair & Maintenance Carrier):
Unicorn.

Oilers:
Brown Ranger, Dingledale, San Ambrosio, Cedardale, Arndale, San Adolpho, Wave King, Aase Maersk.

Naval Store Issuing Ship:
Bacchus.

Victualling Vessels:
Denbighshire, Fort Alabama, City of Dieppe.

Distilling Ship:
Stagpool.

Netlayer:
Guardian.

Armament Issuing Ships:
Corinda, Darvel, Hermelin, Heron, Kheti, Pacheco, Prince de Liege, Princess Maria Pia, Robert Maersk, Thyras.

Hospital Ship:
Tjitualengka.

APPENDIX 2

COMPOSITION OF BPF ON VJ DAY

BATTLESHIPS
    Duke of York   Captain A. D. Nicholl, C.B.E., D.S.O.

King George V	Captain B. B. Schofield, C.B.E.
Anson	Captain A. C. G. Madden.
Howe	Captain H. W. U. McCall, D.S.O.

FLEET and LIGHT CARRIERS

Formidable	Captain W. G. Andrewes, C.B.E., D.S.O.
Indefatigable	Captain Q. D. Graham, C.B.E., D.S.O.
Indomitable	Captain J. A. S. Eccles, C.B.E.
Colossus	Captain G. H. Strokes, C.B., D.S.C.
Glory	Captain A. W. Buzzard, D.S.O., O.B.E.
Venerable	Captain W. A. Dallmeyer, D.S.O.
Illustrious	Captain W. D. Stephens. (En route for England.)
Implacable	Captain C. C. Hughes-Hallet, C.B.E. (Not on station.)
Victorious	Rear-Admiral M. M. Denny, C.B., C.B.E.

ESCORT CARRIERS (Replenishment)

Striker	Captain W. P. Carne.
Arbiter	Captain D. H. Everett, D.S.O., M.B.E.
Chaser	Captain R. G. Poole.
Ruler	Captain H. P. Currey, O.B.E.
Slinger	Lt.-Cdr. J. G. Hopkins.
Speaker	A/Captain U. H. R. Jones.

ESCORT CARRIERS (Ferry)

Vindex	A/Commander J. D. L. Williams, D.S.C.
Fencer	Lt.-Cdr. A. M. Harris. (Not on station.)
Reaper	Commander I. T. Clark, O.B.E. (Not on station.)

LIGHT CRUISERS

Bermuda	Captain J. S. Bethell, C.B.E.
Belfast	Captain R. M. Dick, C.B.E., D.S.C.
Euryalus	Captain R. S. Warne, C.B.E.
Gambia (RNZN)	Captain R. A. B. Edwards, C.B.E.
Achilles (RNZN)	Captain F. J. Butler, M.B.E.
Swiftsure	Captain P. V. McLaughlin.
Argonaut	Captain W. P. McCarthy.
Newfoundland	Captain R. W. Ravenhill, C.B.E., D.S.C.
Black Prince	Captain G. V. Gladstone. (Not on station.)
Ontario (RCN)	Captain H. T. W. Grant, D.S.O., R.C.N. (En route to station.)
Uganda (RCN)	Captain E. R. Mainguy, O.B.E., R.C.N. (Not on station.)

FAST MINELAYERS

Apollo	Captain L. N. Brownfield.
Ariadne	Captain F. F. Lloyd, o.b.e.
Manxman	Captain G. Thistleton-Smith.

AUXILIARY A/A SHIP (RCN)

Prince Robert (RCN)	Captain W. B. Creasey, r.c.n.

DESTROYER DEPOT SHIPS

Montclare	A/Captain G. W. Hoare-Smith.
Tyne	Captain S. Bucher.

FLEET DESTROYERS

D.13. *Napier*	A/Captain H. J. Buchanan, d.s.o., r.a.n.
D.14. *Nepal*	Lt.-Cdr. C. J. Stephenson, r.a.n. (7th DF-RAN)
D.15. *Nizam*	Cdr. C. H. Brooks, r.a.n.
D.16. *Norman*	Lt.-Cdr. J. Plunkett-Cole, r.a.n.
D.22. *Quilliam*	Lt. J. R. Stephens.
D.17. *Quadrant*	Lt.-Cdr. P. C. Hopkins.
D.18. *Quality*	Cdr. Viscount Jocelyn. (4th DF)
D.19. *Queenborough*	Cdr. P. L. Saumarez, d.s.c.
D.20. *Quiberon* (RAN)	Cdr. G. S. Stewart, r.a.n.
D.21. *Quickmatch* (RAN)	Lt.-Cdr. O. H. Becker, d.s.c., r.a.n.
D.49. *Troubridge*	Captain G. F. Burghard.
D.45. *Teazer*	Lt.-Cdr. T. F. Taylor, d.s.c.
D.46. *Tenacious*	Lt.-Cdr. G. C. Crowley, d.s.c. (24th DF)
D.48. *Terpsichore*	Cdr. R. T. White, d.s.o.
D.50. *Tumult*	Lt.-Cdr. A. S. Pomeroy, d.s.c.
D.51. *Tuscan*	Lt.-Cdr. P. B. N. Lewis, d.s.c.
D.52. *Tyrian*	Cdr. R. H. Mills.
D.47. *Termagant*	Lt.-Cdr. D. C. Beatty, d.s.c.
D.11. *Grenville*	Captain R. G. Onslow, d.s.o.
D.23. *Ulster*	Lt.-Cdr. R. J. Hanson, d.s.o., d.s.c. (En route for UK.)
D.24. *Ulysses*	Lt.-Cdr. P. J. Bordes, d.s.c.
D.25. *Undaunted*	Lt.-Cdr. C. E. R. Sharp. (25th DF)
D.26. *Undine*	Cdr. T. C. Robinson, d.s.c.
D.27. *Urania*	Lt.-Cdr. D. H. P. Gardiner, d.s.c.
D.28. *Urchin*	Lt.-Cdr. A. F. Harkness, o.b.e., d.s.c., r.d., r.n.r.
D.29. *Ursa*	Cdr. D. B. Wyburd, d.s.o., d.s.c.
D.12. *Kempenfelt*	Captain E. G. McGregor, d.s.o.
D.31. *Wakeful*	Lt.-Cdr. G. D. Pound, d.s.c.
D.34. *Whirlwind*	Cdr. W. A. F. Hawkins, d.s.o., o.b.e., d.s.c. (27th DF)
D.32. *Wessex*	Lt.-Cdr. R. Horncastle.

D.30. *Wager*	Lt.-Cdr. R. C. Watkin.
D.33. *Whelp*	Cdr. G. A. Norfolk.
D.35. *Wizard*	Lt.-Cdr. R. H. Hodgkinson, D.S.C.
D.36. *Wrangler*	Lt.-Cdr. E. G. Warren.
D.73. *Armada*	Lt.-Cdr. R. A. Fell.
D.61. *Barfleur*	Cdr. M. S. Townsend. (19th DF. Only *Barfleur* on station others en route in Med.)
D.62. *Camperdown*	Lt.-Cdr. J. J. S. Yorke.
D.75. *Trafalgar*	Captain A. F. Pugsley.
D.70. *Penn*	Lt.-Cdr. A. H. Diack. (Damaged off Burma, allocated BPF as Aircraft Target Ship.)
G.68. *Lewes*	Lt.-Cdr. M. H. Grylle. (Old ex-US boat allocated to BPF as Aircraft Target Ship.) Both off station.
Algonquin (RCN)	A/Lt.-Cdr. D. W. Piers, D.S.C., R.C.N.

ESCORT VESSELS (Frigates, Sloops, etc.)

Pheasant	A/Cdr. J. B. Palmer.
Crane	Lt.-Cdr. R. J. Jenkins, D.S.C.
Redpole	Lt.-Cdr. E. J. Lee.
Whimbrel	Lt.-Cdr. N. R. Murch.
Woodcock	A/Lt.-Cdr. S. J. Parsons, D.S.C.
Avon	A/Cdr. P. G. A. King, D.S.C., R.D., R.N.R.
Findhorn	T/A/Lt.-Cdr. J. P. Burnett, R.N.V.R.
Parret	Lt.-Cdr. T. Hood, R.N.R.
Helford	Cdr. C. G. Cuthbertson, D.S.C., R.D., R.N.R.
Barle	T/A/Lt.-Cdr. J. Duncan, D.S.C., R.N.R.
Derg	Lt.-Cdr. N. P. J. Stapleton, R.D., R.N.R.
Odzani	A/Lt.-Cdr. J. N. Burgess, R.A.N.V.R.
Plym	A/Lt.-Cdr. A. Foxall, R.N.R.
Usk	T/A/Lt.-Cdr. G. B. Medlycott, R.N.R.
Widemouth Bay	A/Lt.-Cdr. J. H. MacAlister, R.N.V.R.
Bigbury Bay	A/Lt.-Cdr. G. P. D. Hall, D.S.C.
Veryan Bay	Lt. J. S. Brownrigg, D.S.C.
Whitesand Bay	A/Lt.-Cdr. B. C. Longbottom.
Alacrity	Lt.-Cdr. J. Chatton-Baker, D.S.C.
Amethyst	Lt.-Cdr. N. Scott-Eliot, D.S.C.
Black Swan	Lt.-Cdr. A. D. Inglis.
Erne	Lt.-Cdr. P. S. Evans.
Hart	A/Cdr. H. F. G. Leftwich. (All en route to station.)
Hind	Lt.-Cdr. A. D. White, R.D., R.N.R.
Cygnet	Lt.-Cdr. A. H. Pierce, O.B.E., R.N.R.
Flamingo	Lt. A. Traill, R.N.R.

Opossum	Lt.-Cdr. E. F. Hollins.
Starling	T/A/Lt.-Cdr. G. C. Julian, R.N.Z.N.
Stork	Lt.-Cdr. D. E. Mansfield, D.S.C.
Wren	Cdr. S. R. J. Woods, D.S.C., R.D., R.N.R.

SUBMARINES
(Operationally under BPF)

Taciturn, Tapir, Taurus, Thorough, Thule, Tiptoe, Trenchant, Totem, Trump, Turpin, Terrapin, Tudor, Scotsman, Seascout, Selene, Sidon, Sleuth, Solent, Spearhead, Stubborn, Supreme, Sanguine, Sea Devil, Sea Nymph, Spark, Stygian.

(For A/S Training)

Voracious, Vox, Virtue.

MINESWEEPERS
(Temporarily attached to BPF. None on station VJ Day)

Coquette, Rowena, Mary Rose, Moon, Providence, Seabear, Thisbe, Courier, Felicity, Hare, Liberty, Michael, Minstrel, Wave, Welcome.

FLEET TRAIN

Danlayers: *Shillay;* and *Trodday.*

Boom Carriers: *Fernmoor;* and *Leonian.*

Landing Ships: *Lothian;* and *Glenearn.*

Fleet Accommodation Ships: *Aorangi;* and *Lancashire.*

Repair Ships: *Artifex; Resource; Berry Head; Flamborough Head; Dullisk Cove; Assistance; Diligence; Springdale; Kelantan* (RNZN) and *Arbutus* (RNZN).

Command Ship, Logistics Supply Group: *Aire.*

Air Maintenance Ships: *Pioneer; Unicorn;* and *Deer Sound.*

Aircraft Store Ships: *Fort Colville;* and *Fort Langley.*

Fleet Oilers: *Olna; Arndale; Bishopdale; Cedardale; Eaglesdale; Wave Emperor; Wave Governor; Wave King; Wave Monarch; Brown Ranger; Green Ranger; Rapidol;* and *Serbol* (All RN or RFA).

Aase Maersk; Carelia; San Adolpho; San Amado; San Ambrosio; Darst Creek; Golden Meadow; Iere; Loma Nova; and *Seven Sisters.*

Water Carriers: *Empire Crest;* and *Vacport.*

Distilling Ships: *Bacchus* (RFA); and *Stagpool.*

Netlayer: *Guardian.*

Salvage Vessels: *King Salvor; Salvestor;* and *Salvictor.*

Hospital Ships: *Empire Clyde; Gerusalemme; Maunganui; Oxfordshire; Tjitalengka;* and *Vasna.*

Store Ships: *Corinda; Darvel; Hermelin; Heron; Kheti; Kistna; Pacheco; Prince de Liege; Princess Maria Pia; Robert Maersk; Thyra S; Hickory Burn; Hickory Dale;*

Hickory Glen; Hickory Stream; City of Dieppe; Fort Alabama; Fort Constantine; Fort Dunvegan; Fort Edmonton; Fort Wrangell; Prome; Gudrun Maersk; Kola; Bosporus; Jaarstroom; Marudu; San Andres; Schlesvig; Fort Providence; and Edna (Collier).

Escort HQ Ship: *Enchantress*.

Submarine Depot Ships: *Adamant; Maidstone; and Bonaventure*.

Minesweepers (RAN): *Ballarat; Bendigo; Burnie; Goulburn; Maryborough; Toowoomba; Whyalla; Cessnock; Gawler; Geraldton; Ipswich; Launceston; Pirie; Tamworth; Woolongong; Kalgoorlie; Lismore; and Cairns.*

APPENDIX 3

FLEET AIR ARM SQUADRONS

Squadron	Aircraft	Carrier[1]
801	Seafire	*Implacable*
802	Seafire	*Vengeance*
809	Seafire	*Unicorn*
820	Avenger	*Indefatigable*
828	Avenger	*Implacable*
832	Avenger	*Illustrious*
848	Avenger	*Formidable*
849	Avenger	*Victorious*
854	Avenger	*Illustrious*
857	Avenger	*Indomitable*
880	Seafire	*Implacable*
885	Seafire	*Formidable*
887	Seafire	*Implacable*
888	Hellcat	*Indefatigable*
892	Hellcat	*Ocean*
894	Seafire	*Indefatigable*
897	Seafire	*Unicorn*
899	Seafire	*Indomitable*
1770	Firefly	*Indefatigable*
1771	Firefly	*Implacable*
1772	Firefly	*Indefatigable*
1790	Firefly	*Implacable*
1830	Corsair	*Illustrious*

[1] Many, if not all, front line FAA squadrons were embarked in several different carriers during 1944–45 according to operational requirements; a number were also embarked aboard Escort Carriers of the Fleet Support. This table is therefore only a rough guide to the Air Complements of the BPF Fast Carrier Group.

1831	Corsair	*Vengeance*
1833	Corsair	*Illustrious*
1834	Corsair	*Victorious*
1836	Corsair	*Victorious*
1837	Corsair	*Illustrious*
1839	Hellcat	*Indomitable*
1840	Hellcat	*Formidable*
1841	Corsair	*Formidable*
1842	Corsair	*Formidable*
1844	Hellcat	*Indomitable*
1845	Corsair	*Formidable*
1846	Corsair	*Colossus*
1850	Corsair	*Vengeance*
1851	Corsair	*Venerable*

APPENDIX 4

JAPANESE AIRCRAFT TYPES

In general, the American classification of Japanese aircraft allocated boys' names to fighters and girls' names to bombers so as to avoid any confusion of the two types; these American codenames were used throughout Task Force 57 and are therefore also used throughout the text of this book.

BETTY Mitsubishi *G4M 1* and *G4M 2* Navy Type 1 Land Attack Plane. 6/7-seater land-based bomber.

DINAH Mitsubishi *Ki 46* Army Type 100 Command Reconnaissance Plane. 3-seater fighter/ground attack potential low-wing monoplane.

FRANCES Yokosuka *P1Y 1* and *P1Y 1s* 'Milky Way' Navy Model 11 Land-based Bomber. 3-seater mid-wing monoplane 'white light' night-fighter, bomber, torpedo-bomber or dive-bomber.

JILL Nakajima *B6N 1* and *B6N 2* 'Heavenly Mountain' Navy Models 11 and 12 Carrier-borne Attack Plane. 3-seater mid-wing torpedo and reconnaissance monoplane.

JUDY Yokosuka *D4Y 1* and *D4Y 1c* 'Comet' Navy Type 2 Model 11 Carrier-borne 2-seater Bomber/Reconnaissance plane.

KATE   Nakajima *BSN 1* and *BSN 2* Navy Type 97 Models 11, 12 and 21 Carrier-borne Attack Plane. 2/3-seater torpedo-bomber monoplane.

OSCAR   Nakajima *Ki 43* 'Peregrine Falcon' Army Type 1 Single-seater Fighter Monoplane.

TOJO   Nakajima *Ki 44* 'Demon' Army Type 2 Single-seater Heavy-interceptor Fighter Monoplane.

VAL   Aichi *D3A 1* and *D3A 2* Navy Type 99 Models 11, 22 and 31 Carrier-borne 2-seater low-wing monoplane fixed undercarriage Dive-bomber.

ZEKE (or ZERO)   Mitsubishi *O* Navy Type Single-seater Fighter. There were many variations including a suicide version or Kamikaze.

Index

203

Index

Sea Hurricane, British Naval Fighter, 27.
Servaes, Rear-Admiral R. M., 79, 189.
Sextant Conference, 58.
Shah, H.M. Escort Carrier, 72.
Shima, Vice-Admiral, 64, 65, 66.
Singapore Naval Base, 31, 32, 35.
Slinger, H.M. Escort Carrier, 123.
Soerabaya, attack on, 73.
Somerville, Admiral Sir James, 27, 28, 29, 72, 73, 75, 76, 179.
Songei Gerong, target in Palembang attacks, 84, 95, 96, 97, 98.
South Dakota, U.S. Battleship, 184.
Speaker, H.M. Escort Carrier, 116, 117, 132, 134, 148, 154.
'Special Attack Forces', Japanese anti-shipping air squadrons, 85; attack fleet, 99; wiped out, 100.
Spruance, Admiral, 80, 156, 161, 167.
Stalin, Marshal Josef, 191.
Stirling, Sub-Lieutenant Ian, 140.
Striker, H.M. Escort Carrier, 116, 117, 121, 140, 150.
Suffolk, H.M. Heavy Cruiser, 81.
Swiftsure, H.M. Light Cruiser, 116, 117, 127, 137, 139, 149, 163, 164, 165, 189.

Takao, Japanese Heavy Cruiser, 65.
Talangbetoetoe Airfield, 85, 90.
Takuanan Maru 6, Japanese Auxiliary, 184.
Taylor, P/O A.N., 97, 98.
Teazer, H.M. Destroyer, 163, 164, 167, 186.
Tenacious, H.M. Destroyer, 150, 151, 156, 163, 164, 167, 184, 186.
Termagant, H.M. Destroyer, 154, 156, 163, 164, 167, 184, 186.
Terpsichore, H.M. Destroyer, 163, 164, 167, 184.
Tirpitz, German Battleship, 38, 53, 54, 155.
Togo, Admiral, 20.
Tromp, Dutch Light Cruiser, 73, 75, 76.
Troubridge, H.M. Destroyer, 150, 152, 156, 163, 164, 186.
Tumult, H.M. Destroyer, 189.
Turkey, U.S. Naval Tug, 154.
Tuscan, H.M. Destroyer, 189.
Tyrian, H.M. Destroyer, 189.

Ugaaki, Admiral, 188.
Uganda, H.M. Light Cruiser, 130, 137, 149, 163, 164, 165, 167.
Ulster, H.M. Destroyer, 116, 126, 137.
Ulysses, H.M. Destroyer, 167, 181, 182.
Umezu, Japanese General, 189.

Undaunted, H.M. Destroyer, 86, 116, 130, 134, 137, 140, 167.
Undine, H.M. Destroyer, 86, 116, 120, 137, 167, 181, 182.
Unicorn, H.M. Aircraft-Carrier, 72, 78.
Urania, H.M. Destroyer, 116, 129, 132, 137, 167, 181, 182, 189.
Urchin, H.M. Destroyer, 86, 89, 130, 137, 167.
Ursa, H.M. Destroyer, 86, 93, 100, 116, 130, 137, 189.

Valiant, H.M. Battleship, 39, 72, 75.
Vanguard, H.M. Battleship, 53.
Vaughan, Surgeon-Lieutenant, 123.
Venerable, H.M. Aircraft-Carrier, 188, 189.
Vengeance, H.M. Aircraft-Carrier, 188, 189.
Vian, Admiral Sir Philip, 58, 77, 78, 79, 81, 93, 98, 113, 121, 133, 134, 137, 144, 147, 148, 155, 161, 166, 167, 178, 179, 180.
Victorious, H.M. Aircraft-Carrier, 39, 72, 75, 77, 81, 86, 93, 95, 98, 100, 116, 123, 136, 139, 140, 144, 145, 146, 151, 152, 167, 174, 175, 177, 178, 183, 189.

Wager, H.M. Destroyer, 79, 86, 116, 118, 121, 122, 137.
Wakeful, H.M. Destroyer, 79, 86, 176, 186.
Walker, Admiral, 189.
Walker, Captain, 50.
Warspite, H.M. Battleship, 27.
Washington, Naval Conference and Treaty, 21, 22, 31.
Wasp, U.S. Carrier, 78.
Wave King, R.F.A., 79, 86, 140, 150, 151, 153.
Wave Monarch, R.F.A., 140, 150, 153.
Weasel, Tug, 148, 152, 153, 154.
Wessex, H.M. Destroyer, 79, 86, 116, 132, 137, 140, 149, 154.
Whelp, H.M. Destroyer, 79, 86, 97, 116, 117, 121, 130, 137.
Whimbrel, H.M. Sloop, 140, 152.
Whirlwind, H.M. Destroyer, 79, 86, 116, 117, 121, 130, 137, 154, 189.
Whylla, R.N.Z.N., 148.
Wilhelm II, Kaiser of Germany, 19.
Woodcock, H.M. Sloop, 151.
Wrangler, H.M. Destroyer, 79, 176, 186.

Yahagi, Japanese Light Cruiser, 128.
Yamamato, Admiral, 29.
Yamato, Japanese Battleship, 38, 41, 128, 154.